PHL

D1339514

Before Color Prejudice

THE
PAUL HAMLYN
LIBRARY

DONATED BY
THE PAUL HAMLYN
FOUNDATION
TO THE
BRITISH MUSEUM

opened December 2000

BEFORE COLOR PREJUDICE

The Ancient View
of Blacks

Frank M. Snowden, Jr.

Harvard University Press
Cambridge, Massachusetts
London, England

Copyright © 1983 by the President and Fellows of Harvard College
All rights reserved
Printed in the United States of America
Sixth printing, 1997

First Harvard University Press paperback edition, 1991

Library of Congress Cataloging in Publication Data

Snowden, Frank M., 1911-
    Before color prejudice.

    Includes index.
    1. Race relations—History.   2. Intercultural
communication.   3. Blacks in art.   4. Civilization,
Ancient.   I. Title.
GN496.S65   1983   305.8′96   82-11852
ISBN 0-674-06380-5 (cloth)
ISBN 0-674-06381-3 (paper)

THE
BRITISH
MUSEUM
THE PAUL HAMLYN LIBRARY

305.89603SNO

uxori carissimae

PREFACE

The encounter of African blacks and Mediterranean whites consti-
tutes the oldest chapter in the annals of black-white relations. A
record of these meetings is reliably attested for the first time in
Egyptian documents about the middle of the third millennium B.C.,
and black-white contacts engaged the attention of artists and
chroniclers in the Egyptian, Greek, and Roman worlds at various
times thereafter until the sixth century A.D. Though certain aspects
of these relations have been the subject of recent studies, there is no
comprehensive study of the image of blacks in the minds of the
Mediterranean whites who opposed them in battle or lived with
them in peace during the period from the Pharaohs to the Caesars.
Nor have the reasons for the absence of bitter antagonism toward
blacks in the ancient world been adequately examined.

The aim of this book is twofold: through a study of the iconographical and written sources, to trace the image of blacks as seen by
whites from Egyptian to Roman times, and to explore the rationale
for the attitude toward blacks during this period. The very striking
similarities in the total picture that emerge from an examination of
the basic sources—Egyptian, Greek, Roman, and early Christian—
point to a highly favorable image of blacks and to white-black relationships differing markedly from those that have developed in
more color-conscious societies. I have given special attention to
modern misreadings of the ancient evidence which have frequently
resulted from a failure to take into consideration relevant research
in the social sciences. Commentators, for example, have sometimes
indicted the ancients for color prejudice merely because they manifested some general tendencies common to most people, Negroes

included. The use of pertinent findings in the social sciences, especially on the origin and nature of color prejudice, and the examination of the image of blacks in later societies have proved valuable in deepening my understanding of color and race in antiquity, and have perhaps brought fresh perspectives to a subject of interest to students of both the ancient and the modern world.

In the preparation of this book, I have received valuable assistance from many. I have benefited greatly from the constructive suggestions of the scholars who read an earlier version of Chapter Four—Professors David Brion Davis, Mason Hammond, John Higham, and Bernard M. W. Knox; for any errors of fact or judgment I am, of course, responsible. I acknowledge my gratitude to the institutions that provided time for research and writing. A grant from the National Endowment for the Humanities in 1970 enabled me to deepen my knowledge of ancient Roman northwest Africa. My sabbatical leave from Howard University in 1977–78 was spent as a Fellow of the Woodrow Wilson International Center for Scholars at the Smithsonian Institution in Washington, D.C. In October–November 1977, I was Resident Scholar at the Rockefeller Bellagio Study and Conference Center in Italy. I want to express my appreciation to Howard University for financial assistance at various stages of my research. My thanks go to scores of individuals and museums for the courtesy of providing photographs and permission to publish them, and for their kindness in helping me study objects in their collections. The Menil Foundation has been especially gracious in allowing me to reproduce photographs and to adapt maps from *The Image of the Black in Western Art.*

CONTENTS

Before Color Prejudice

1

WHO WERE THE AFRICAN BLACKS?

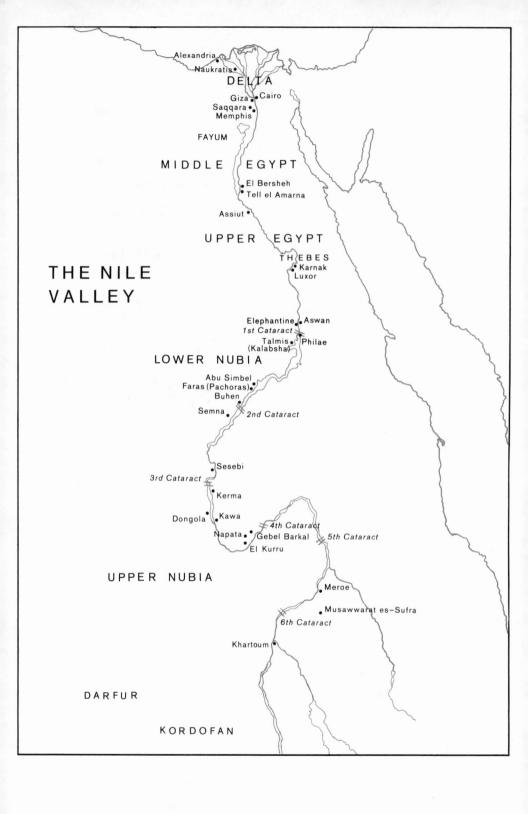

1

The dark- and black-skinned Africans mentioned most often in the records of Mediterranean peoples lived in parts of the Nile Valley south of the First Cataract. This region was designated frequently in Egyptian texts and the Old Testament as Kush (Cush) and as Aithiopia (Aethiopia) in Greek, Roman, and early Christian authors.[1] The area, also referred to as Nubia, is often divided into Lower Nubia, extending from the First to the Second Cataract; and Upper Nubia, stretching southward from the Second Cataract to the area in the vicinity of Meroë, situated about halfway between the Fifth Cataract and present-day Khartoum.[2]

For the land and peoples of the Nile Valley south of Egypt, I have in general used Kush and Kushites for periods covered by Egyptian or Assyrian documents and the Old Testament; and Ethiopia and Ethiopians when I cite Greek, Roman, and Christian sources. I have also followed a common practice in using Nubia and Nubians as general terms for the region and its inhabitants. In the interest of clarity I have sometimes used Napatans for Nubians of the Napatan Kingdom of Kush (ca. 750–300 B.C.) when the royal burial ground was located at Napata, near the Fourth Cataract, and Meroïtes for the people of the Meroïtic Kingdom of Kush (ca. 300 B.C. to 350 A.D.), after the royal cemetery had been moved farther south to Meroë.[3]

Several peoples described as Ethiopians or by other words indicating degrees of blackness are reported to have lived also in various parts of northwest Africa. In this region of Africa there was ro precise geographical landmark corresponding to the First Cataract that divided areas occupied by whites and blacks.[4] The evidence, however, suggests that blacks in northwest Africa for the most part inhabited the southern fringes, extending roughly from perhaps the oasis of Ammon (Siwa), but at least from the present-day Fezzan and the oases of southern Tunisia to the Atlantic coast of southern

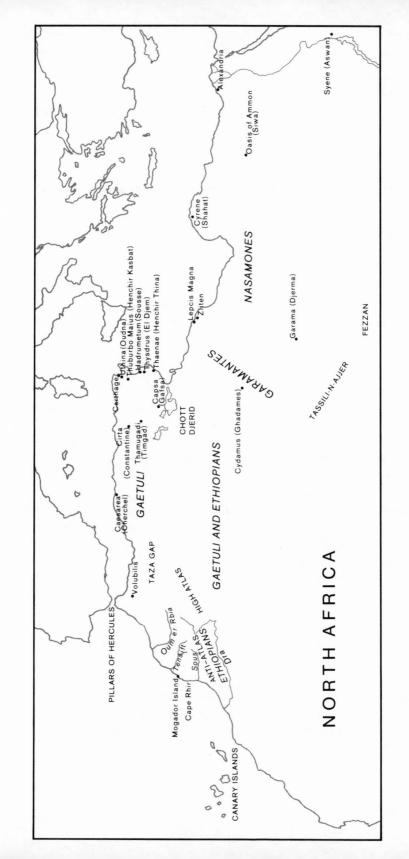

NORTH AFRICA

PILLARS OF HERCULES

Volubilis

TAZA GAP

Capsarea
(Cherchel)

GAETULI

Cirta
(Constantine)

Thamugadi
(Timgad)

Carthage

Uthina (Oudna)
Thuburbo Maius (Henchir Kasbat)
Hadrumetum (Sousse)
Thysdrus (El Djem)
Thaenae (Henchir Thina)

Capsa
Gafsa

CHOTT
DJERID

GAETULI AND ETHIOPIANS

HIGH ATLAS

Oum er Rbia
Tensift
Sous
ANTI-ATLAS
Dra

ETHIOPIANS

Mogador Island

Cape Rhir

CANARY ISLANDS

Lepcis Magna
Zliten

Cyrene
(Shahat)

NASAMONES

GARAMANTES

Cydamus (Ghadames)

TASSILI-N-AJJER

Garama (Djerma)

FEZZAN

Oasis of Ammon
(Siwa)

Alexandria

Syene (Aswan)

Morocco; and blacks at times lived in areas closer to the Mediterranean littoral.[5] Blacks who found their way to other countries of
the ancient world outside Africa came for the most part from regions of the Nile Valley, but also, especially during the Roman period, to some extent from northwest Africa.

Scholars differ in their views as to the proper anthropological
classification of the African blacks known to the ancient world. The
question of an appropriate designation for these blacks is further
complicated by changing modern usage, according to which dark-
and black-skinned peoples have been described at different times as
"colored, "Negro," or "black." The ancients themselves, however, in
realistic portraits and detailed descriptions, have provided perhaps
the best picture of the physical characteristics of African blacks.

Color in the Nomenclature of Blacks

The so-called pure or pronounced Negroid type—blacks with broad
noses, thick lips, and tightly coiled or woolly hair—appears in
Egyptian art as early as the latter part of the third millennium B.C.[6]
Yet Egyptian inscriptions and literature rarely mention the color of
the Kushites, refer only occasionally to the southerners' curly hair,
and never provide detailed physical descriptions of blacks like
those of later Greek and Roman authors.[7] The word Nehesyu, used
in Egyptian texts to designate settled inhabitants of the Nile Valley
south of Egypt, did not, like the classical term Aethiopian, emphasize color but seems to have been derived from a place name.[8] A
partial explanation of this may lie in the fact that from earliest
times Egyptians had been acquainted with blacks, had fought
alongside black mercenaries at least as early as 2000 B.C.,[9] and
hence, as a result of a longstanding familiarity, saw nothing unusual
in the Kushites' color or their other physical characteristics.

Reactions to African blackness, however, differed in other areas
of the Mediterranean world, where blacks had not been, as in
Egypt, a familiar part of the daily scene. Upon their first introduction to blacks, whites outside Africa were obviously struck by the
novelty of the Africans' skin. The color of the Nubians became proverbial. "Can the Ethiopian change his skin or the leopard his

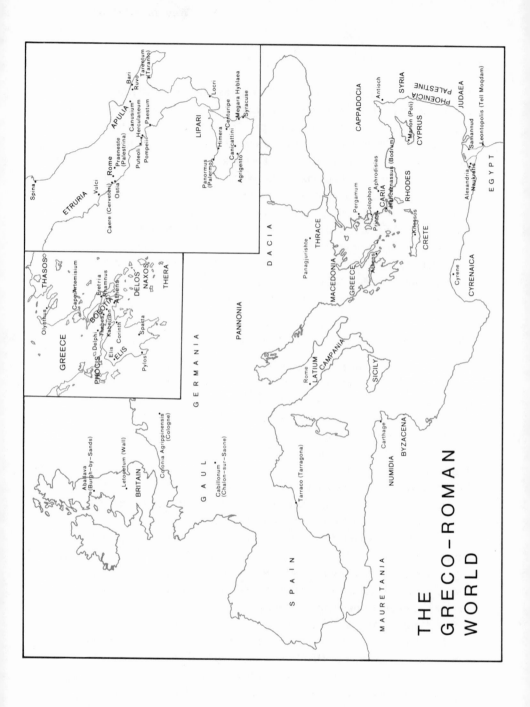

THE GRECO-ROMAN WORLD

spots?" asked Jeremiah, apparently well acquainted with the color of Africans since it was a Kushite, Ebed-melech, who had interceded on behalf of the prophet when he was imprisoned in the palace of Zedekiah.[10] "To wash an Ethiopian white" was a common expression in the Greek and Roman world, used to describe futile labors or to illustrate the unchangeability of nature.[11]

Among the Greeks and Romans who have provided the fullest descriptions of blacks, the Africans' color was regarded as their most characteristic and most unusual feature. In this respect the ancients were not unlike whites of later generations who used color terms as a kind of shorthand to denote Africans and those of African descent. The Arab historian Ibn Khaldûn made a pertinent comment on this practice when he observed that whites did not designate inhabitants of the north, like those of the south, by their color because "whiteness was something usual and common (to them), and they did not see anything sufficiently remarkable in it to cause them to use it as a specific term."[12] The Greeks, followed by the Romans, were the first of many peoples to apply to blacks, or their country, names emphasizing color—Ethiopians, Negroes, blacks, colored peoples, Bilād al-Sūdān (land of the blacks), l'Afrique Noire. *Aithiops* (*Aethiops*), the most common generic term in the Greek and Roman world applied to blacks from the south of Egypt and from the southern fringes of northwest Africa, highlighted the color of the skin. The word meant literally a "burnt-faced person," a "colored" person from certain regions of Africa, and in origin was a reflection of the environment theory that attributed the Ethiopians' color as well as their tightly coiled hair to the intense heat of the southern sun.[13]

Ethiopians became the yardstick by which classical antiquity measured colored peoples. In the early first century A.D. Manilius in his poem on astrology mentioned the groups who were to be included most frequently in a familiar classical "color scheme": Ethiopians, the blackest; Indians, less sunburned; Egyptians, mildly dark; and the Mauri (Moors), whose name was derived from the color of their skin.[14] The Indians whom Alexander visited were said to be blacker than all other peoples except Ethiopians; those south of the Ganges were described as browned by the sun but not so black as Ethiopians; northern Indians resembled Egyptians.[15]

All blacks, however, did not look alike to the Greeks and Romans, who made careful note of differences in the Ethiopians' pigmentation. Ethiopians were not of the same color, varying from dark (*fusci*) to very black (*nigerrimi*).[16] The Acridophagi (Locust Eaters) were described by Agatharchides and Diodorus as exceedingly black.[17] People living in the vicinity of Meroë, according to Ptolemy, were deeply black in color and pure Ethiopians.[18] The region in the neighborhood of the Egyptian–Nubian boundary, however, was inhabited by people who, according to Flavius Philostratus, were not completely black but half-breeds in color, not so black as Ethiopians but darker than Egyptians.[19] In short, classical descriptions of gradations in the skin color of blacks in the Nile Valley compare favorably with the observations of modern anthropologists such as B. G. Trigger's: "On an average, between the Delta in northern Egypt and the Sudd of the Upper Nile, skin color tends to darken from light brown to what appears to the eye as bluish black."[20]

The nomenclature and descriptions of blacks in northwest Africa also underscore the attentive detail of Greek and Roman observers. Several peoples from this area of Africa were specifically designated as Ethiopians by one or more ancient authors.[21] Blackness was an emphasis in the names of certain tribes such as the Nigritae and Erebidae (children of darkness).[22] Very black auxiliaries, according to Frontinus, were among the Carthaginian prisoners taken by Gelon of Syracuse in 480 B.C.[23] A number of descriptions of north African blacks reflect efforts to describe coloration accurately: the body of a slave from Hadrumetum (in southern Tunisia) was described as pitch-black; the fame of a black athlete Olympius evoked from the sixth-century poet Luxorius a laudatory multiple image of blackness; in his account of the triumph of Justinian's general John Troglita over rebellious Moors, the African poet Corippus mentions captives black as crows.[24] In a letter addressed to Fulgentius, bishop of Ruspe (in Byzacena, southern Tunisia) in the sixth century, a young black convert to Christianity was said to be Ethiopian in color and from the most distant part of a region where men are darkened by the dry heat of the fiery sun.[25]

Several other peoples of northwest Africa were apparently regarded as a kind of intermediate population, an amalgam of white and Ethiopian. Such a classification, for example, is strongly suggested by the nomenclature of several elements in the population of northwest Africa: the Melanogaetuli (black Gaetuli) and the Leukaethiopes (white Ethiopians), the former a major and the latter a minor people of inner Libya, according to Ptolemy, and the Libyoaethiopes (Libyan Ethiopians) mentioned by Orosius.[26] Similarly, Diodorus was perhaps indicating racial mixture by his statement that the Asphodelodes, captured by a lieutenant of Agathocles at the end of the fourth century B.C., resembled Ethiopians in color.[27]

The Garamantes, who are believed to have lived in the area of the modern Fezzan, were classified by some authors as Ethiopians but were distinguished from Ethiopians by others.[28] Very dark in color, these northwest Africans were described by Lucan as sunburned (perusti); by Arnobius as swarthy (furvi); and by Ptolemy as moderately black, a hue resembling that of the inhabitants of Triakontaschoinos above Syene.[29] In one instance Ptolemy seems to consider the Garamantes as Ethiopians when he states that they had the same king as their neighbors, the inhabitants of inner Ethiopia, but elsewhere he seems to distinguish between Ethiopians and Garamantes.[30] The very dark, curly-haired gladiators in a mosaic of the late first century A.D. from Zliten (east of Lepcis Magna in Libya) have been interpreted as Garamantes.[31] The Mauri, another northwest African people whose color received frequent notice, were at times described as nigri (black) and adusti (scorched).[32] By classifying some Garamantes as Ethiopian, classical writers were evidently aware of Negroid Garamantes. On the other hand, when ancient authors called specific attention only to the color of certain Garamantes and Mauri, and made direct or implied comparisons with Ethiopians, they were perhaps describing racially mixed segments of the population: apparently some Garamantes, those classified as Ethiopian, were Negroid, while others, lighter and less Negroid, were an amalgam of Ethiopian and Garamantian elements; and certain Mauri, darker than the predominantly white Mauri but not as black as Ethiopians, were black-white crosses. As Jehan Desanges has observed, the "Mauri and the Garamante were often looked upon and thought of as being half black."[33]

Physical Features of Blacks

In addition to their observations on color, classical writers commented on the Africans' woolly or tightly coiled hair, the broad, flat nose, the thick, everted lips, and occasionally other traits. Xenophanes, who described Ethiopians as black and flat-nosed, was the first European to apply to Africans a physical characteristic other than color; Herodotus was the first to call attention to the hair of African Ethiopians, the "woolliest" of all mankind.[34] Ethiopians who lived near the Nile, according to Diodorus, were black, flat-nosed, and woolly-haired.[35] The idea that a white man could pass for an Ethiopian merely by blackening his body was ridiculous, Petronius points out, because color alone does not make an Ethiopian: a complete Ethiopian disguise requires several basic modifications in the white man's makeup—in hair, lips, and facial scarification.[36]

Accurate and often detailed information about the black man's physical characteristics is apparent in several classical accounts. Fullness of detail, however, is perhaps best illustrated by the *Moretum*, a poem ascribed to Vergil by ancient authorities, which in only four verses gives the most complete portrait of a black from classical antiquity: "African in race, her whole figure proof of her country—her hair tightly curled, lips thick, color dark, chest broad, breasts pendulous, belly somewhat pinched, legs thin, and feet broad and ample."[37] In this succinct metrical description the author of the *Moretum* delineated several characteristics of the Negroid division of mankind in language remarkably similar to that of modern anthropologists. This interest in the physical appearance of blacks is illustrated further by references of other classical authors to the unusual height of certain Ethiopians,[38] to the Ethiopian practices of circumcision[39] and facial scarification,[40] and to a condition resembling vitiligo.[41]

Blacks as Seen by Ancient Artists

The vast evidence of ancient art is an invaluable source of information concerning the black populations of antiquity. This is not the place for a detailed account of blacks in ancient art, but it is important to call attention to the extensive gallery of blacks depicted by Mediterranean artists at various times from the middle of the third millennium B.C. until late in the Roman Empire. Scholars may differ in their views as to the meaning of ancient terminology for blacks and as to the significance of textual references to coloration and other physical characteristics. There can be little doubt, however, that artists, in their portrayals of Nehesyu, Kushite, or Ethiopian, did depict broad or narrow noses, thin or thick lips, straight or woolly hair. In fact, ancient artists have furnished vivid pictorial definitions of blacks, a kind of anthropological "carte d'identité," and have shown in a variety of media the extent to which individuals with Negroid features were represented in the iconography of the ancient world.

Blacks in Egyptian art

The wife of a prince from the court of Memphis (figs. 1–2) is one of the first clearly recognizable portraits of a black in the history of Egyptian art. Her rather broad nose and thick lips are clearly delineated in a limestone head of about 2600 B.C.[42] Statuettes from the Twelfth Dynasty (ca. 1991–1786 B.C.), like the ivory "doll" (fig. 3) of unknown provenance in New York or the wooden figurine of a "concubine" from el Bersheh in Boston,[43] illustrate the features of other black women depicted by early Egyptian artists. It was, however, primarily black men—soldiers, mercenaries, captives—who served as the subjects for Egyptian artists. Among the limestone heads of prisoners (fig. 4) from the temples of the pyramid of Pepy I (ca. 2423–2300 B.C.) and Pepy II (ca. 2400–2200 B.C.) are those of southerners whose broad noses, thick lips, and hair arranged in parallel rows of tightly coiled braids leave no doubt that these captives were blacks of a pronounced Negroid type.[44] Stelae of black mercenaries (ca. 2180–2040 B.C.) with broad noses, thick lips, and hair edged with dots show that by the beginning of the second millennium blacks and their wives, sometimes Egyptian, were established at Gebelein, near Thebes;[45] and wooden models of forty archers (fig. 5a-b) found in the tomb of a prince (Mesehty) point to the presence of black-skinned recruits farther north at Assiut about 2000 B.C.[46] Though not very numerous, the realistic portrayals of blacks in early Egyptian art are sufficient to illustrate the types of Kushites known to Egyptians prior to the New Kingdom and to show that *Nehesyu,* a word used of southerners as early as 2300 B.C., included peoples with Negroid features.

The much more frequent appearance of blacks in the art of the New Kingdom (ca. 1567–1085 B.C.) was obviously a reflection of in-creased Pharaonic activity in Kush. Artists of the New Kingdom did not completely abandon exact portraiture in delineations of Kush-ites, but Egypt's southern foes, no matter what their origin in Nubia, were often represented with pronounced Negroid features, just as its northern enemies, regardless of country, were stylized whites, with beards and aquiline noses. From about 1400 B.C. on, Egyptian artists often portrayed southerners with dark or intensely black skin, flat noses, thick lips, accentuated prognathism, tightly coiled hair represented by parallel braids, men and women wearing large circular earrings, and women with pendulous breasts. In spite of the prominence of stylized Negroes in the iconography of the New Kingdom, artists nevertheless found their models in African reality (fig. 6).[47] Jean Vercoutter has pointed to the physical characteristics of blacks in scenes from tomb paintings of the New Kingdom as ex-amples of the accurate portrayal of blacks. The tall, slender tribute-bearers in a mural from the tomb of Sebekhotep (ca. 1400 B.C.), re-semble the dolichocephalic Dinkas and Shilluks of today (fig. 7a-b), while the Negroes from the tomb of Huy (ca. 1342–1333 B.C.) suggest the present-day inhabitants of the Nuba mountains (fig. 8a-b).[48]

The Twenty-fifth Dynasty in contemporary art

The sculpture of the Twenty-fifth Dynasty sheds some light on the physical appearance of the people from the Napatan Kingdom of Kush whose rulers of Egypt were called Ethiopians in Greek records. A profile of one of the earliest known kings of the Dynasty, appearing on a sandstone stele from Elephantine, shows the mon-arch Kashta (ca. 760–742 B.C.) with a flat nose and prominent thick lips[49]—characteristics seen also in the portraits of other rulers of the Dynasty, such as Shabaka (ca. 716–702 B.C.; fig. 9). Taharqa (ca.

690–664 B.C.), one of the best known of the Napatan kings, is depicted with a heavy face, fleshy nose, and a thick-lipped mouth (figs. 10–11), and with his flesh painted a dark brown in a fresco from Qaṣr Ibrîm.[50] An "average image" of these Napatans, Jean Leclant has suggested, is perhaps to be found in the numerous representations of divinities such as Amun, Ptah, and Osiris which reflect the royal iconography and provide a generic picture of Napatans "in whom there was often an admixture of Negro blood . . . rather heavy nose, prominent cheekbones, fleshy lips, and powerful chin."[51]

An important record of the Twenty-fifth Dynasty as seen by Mediterranean whites from outside Africa comes from contemporary Assyrian artists. A beautifully carved eighth-century ivory plaquette from Nimrud (fig. 12) shows the royal lion cub about to devour a black, unmistakably Negroid: his lips are thick and his hair is formed from ivory pegs inserted separately.[52] The Napatans are also represented as blacks in monuments celebrating campaigns of two Assyrian monarchs directed against the Twenty-fifth Dynasty. Two kneeling prisoners, one white and one black, portrayed in victory stelae found in Asia, lift their hands in supplication to a towering Esarhaddon (680–669 B.C.).[53] It has been suggested that the white captive in one monument was the king of Tyre and, in the other, the king of Sidon; and that the black, a "pure" Negro, was in both stelae Taharqa or perhaps his heir apparent, Ushanahuru.[54] Blacks are among those appearing in a scene on a bas-relief from the palace of King Ashurbanipal (669–626 B.C.) at Nineveh: warriors manning the pylonlike towers of a besieged city and captives in a procession (fig. 13) led by an Assyrian commander.[55] Whether blacks were included in these Asiatic monuments because they constituted the bulk of the Egyptian-Napatan foe, or because they were the most formidable or merely representative of the opposing army, is not certain. This evidence, however, is important for the light it throws on contemporary views of the black element in the population of the Twenty-fifth Dynasty. The historical value is undeniable—there is no question, as W. S. Smith has emphasized, that in these pieces the sculptor has "correctly observed the physiognomy of men from the Sudan."[56]

Blacks in Mediterranean art outside Africa

The island of Crete has yielded the first blacks portrayed in Mediterranean art beyond Africa. Among the earliest of these is a profile
with very thick lips and snub nose, carved in shell (fig. 14), found in
southern Crete, dating from the early second millennium B.C.[57] A
procession of coal-black warriors appears in a fresco from Cnossos
(ca. 1550–1500 B.C.),[58] and another fresco of approximately the same
period from the island of Thera carries the profile of a black whose
Negroid traits are somewhat reduced—wavy hair, rather thick lips,
and medium-broad nose.[59] Blacks entered the artistic picture of
mainland Greece about the second half of the thirteenth century
B.C. in the fresco from the palace of Nestor at Pylos, which depicts a
procession of blacks and whites in a scene of uncertain meaning—
perhaps offertory, perhaps tributary.[60]

Beginning in the early sixth century B.C. black figures from the
workshops of classical artists became well-known ethnic types in
various parts of the ancient world. Negroes portrayed in several
media have been found notably in Egypt, Greece, Italy, and Sicily
but also in widely scattered regions of the Greek and Roman world
from Letocetum (Wall) and Colonia Agrippinensis (Cologne) in
northern Europe to Thysdrus (El Djem) and Thamugadi (Timgad)
on the southern fringes of Roman northwest Africa, from Tarraco
(Tarragona) in the west to Aphrodisias (in northeast Caria—Tur-
key) in the east.[61]

The first blacks of Greek art were of the pronounced Negroid
type. A faience perfume vase from the first half of the sixth century
B.C., found in Cyprus (fig. 15), contrasts a bearded white and a Negro
with flat nose, thick lips, and hair in the form of diamond-shaped
blocks.[62] Scrupulous attention to detail is strikingly noticeable in
Greek portrayals of blacks from the very beginning. The method of
representing the hair used in the janiform vase from Cyprus was
only one technique employed to render the black man's hair realis-
tically. Raised dots in sixth-century vases in the shape of Negro
heads (fig. 16) give the effect of tightly coiled hair,[63] and the impression of masses of woolly hair is effectively rendered in white on
a fifth-century pelike (fig. 17) on which Andromeda's Negro attendants are outlined on a black background.[64] The designer of sixth-

century terracotta molds from the vicinity of Naukratis (fig. 18) had apparently observed Africans with frontal cicatrices;[65] and, like Herodotus, the painter of a fifth-century pelike from Boeotia (fig. 19) was acquainted with the Ethiopian practice of circumcision.[66]

Mixed black-white types began to appear in Greek art about the middle of the fifth century B.C. Whether prior to this time Greek artists were acquainted primarily with the "pure" Negro, or whether the selection was dictated largely by the first impressions of a newly discovered and vastly different type, is not certain. At any rate, toward the mid-fifth century mulattoes (figs. 20–21) appeared: Busiris and his followers,[67] attendants of Andromeda, Cepheus, a personification of Ethiopia in a theatrical scene,[68] and a servant in attendance on her mistress.[69] The emergence of mulattoes is another illustration of the manner in which the blacks of the artists, even in mythological scenes, often reflected anthropological reality. Ethiopians who served in Xerxes' invasion of Greece in 480 B.C. were very likely blacks of the pronounced type, resembling those of the early Greek artists. Children of Greek women by Xerxes' Ethiopian soldiers would have been mixed, with reduced Negroid features. It was apparently such mulatto types, often youthful, the "brown babies" of the Persian Wars, which attracted artists before Aristotle, in the next century, illustrated the transmission of physical characteristics in the descendants of black-white racial mixture by citing the families of a white woman from Elis and another from Sicily.[70]

From the third century B.C. on, an extremely wide variety of blacks was depicted with remarkable realism. Some modern specialists have regarded Negroes in Greek and Roman art as repetitions of only a few "typical" or "conventional" blacks, but such opinions underestimate the significance of numerous individualized portraits of blacks, which are in fact merely the surviving examples of many others that must have existed in antiquity. We shall never know precisely how many blacks in the Ptolemaic world had features similar to those of the early third-century terracotta head in the Ashmolean Museum (fig. 22a-b)—strongly everted lips, frontal cicatrices, and tightly coiled hair represented by tiny circular dots incised in the clay; or how many blacks resembled the youth in London (fig. 23), delicately molded in bronze about 100 B.C.—with narrower noses, thinner lips, and hair arranged in corkscrew curls.[71]

There is little doubt, though, that the creators of pieces like these had to have worked from live models.

The highly individualized portraits and the freshness of the tableaux in which blacks appeared often suggest direct personal observation. The bronze bust dating from the second or first century B.C., found at Samannûd in Egypt (fig. 24), which has been described as that of a scornful prisoner of war, reminiscent in its characterization of the Pergamene Gauls, portrays a Negro with carefully delineated features, including a wart on the left cheek.[72] The second-century A.D. marble head of a young mulatto girl from Corinth (fig. 25a-b) is the type of portrait expected from an artist who could have had the opportunity to observe blacks in early Christian Corinth (whose presence there has been attested by anthropological evidence).[73] Residents of Campania in the first century A.D. would have readily recognized the authenticity of the Isiac ritual performed by black and white cultists depicted on frescoes from Herculaneum.[74] Scenes such as that on a third-century A.D. mosaic from Thysdrus (El Djem) of a black *venator* (animal fighter) celebrating with colleagues (fig. 26) were doubtless familiar to north Africans acquainted with well-known black athletes like Olympius, the animal fighter, and an invincible charioteer popular with the Carthaginian public of the sixth century.[75]

Characteristics of African Blacks: A Summary

Some scholars have avoided the terms "black" and "Negro" in discussions of African blacks of the ancient world. In describing the prisoners, perhaps Garamantes, appearing in a mosaic of the first century A.D., Jehan Desanges states that the figures are "particularly dark and show Negroid features, although they are not Negroes."[76] B. G. Trigger considers the division of peoples of the Nile Valley into Caucasoid and Negroid stocks "an act that is arbitrary and wholly devoid of historical or biological significance."[77] Nubians, in the judgment of W. Y. Adams, may be described as black or white according to the prejudices of one's time and temperament.[78] On the question of the physical characteristics of African blacks, however, the ancients were far from unclear. As contemporary witnesses of blacks in their own communities, ancient artists deserve more serious attention than they have received. "The image of the black in ancient art," as John Russell has observed, "has a directness, an assurance and a profusion of exact physical detail," and was a product of times "when blacks were taken for granted as neighbors and familiars: in Egypt, above all, but intermittently in the Greco-Roman world and in ancient north Africa as well."[79]

Regardless of modern opinions as to the precise racial identity or proper anthropological classification of Kushites, Nubians, or Ethiopians, the blacks of ancient artists often bear a close similarity to racial types designated in the modern world as "colored," "black," or "Negro" (figs. 27–28). And many of these, had they lived at a later time, would have been regarded as black or Negro and subjected to prejudice because of their color. The colored peoples of both the writers and the artists of antiquity, we have seen, were characterized by various combinations of physical traits—dark or black skin color, thick lips, wide or broad noses, woolly or tightly curled hair—traits used by anthropologists today in classifications of Negroid peoples.[80] The ancients were acquainted with a wide range of types whose physical characteristics were not unlike those of the highly mixed American Negro described by M. J. Herskovits as varying from "the man of dark-brown skin and African appearance to the man who is almost white, and from the broad-nosed, thick-lipped black man to the Caucasoid-looking, thin-lipped, narrow-nosed 'technical' Negro . . . from . . . tightly coiled hair to that of Indian-like straightness."[81]

Following the Greek and Roman practice, I use a color term, "black," as a general designation for the dark- and black-skinned Africans of this study. Like the word "Ethiopian," "black" in my usage properly emphasizes color and includes the colored peoples comprehended by the classical term. At times I use "Negro" or "Negroid" when I have in mind modern anthropological classifications, or persons having at least two of the physical characteristics included in such descriptions. And I designate as mulatto or mixed individuals who, in my judgment or that of others, suggest black-white mixtures of the type described in modern studies.[82]

2

MEETINGS
OF
BLACKS
AND
WHITES

2

The ancient view of blacks was to a great extent a reflection of reality and of the experiences of whites and blacks from Nubia and northwest Africa. The aim of this chapter is not to give a history of blacks and whites in the Mediterranean world, but to present a sketch of major black-white encounters as a background for the understanding of the image of blacks reflected in the written and iconographical records of the Egyptians, Greeks, Romans, and early Christians.

Kushites and Egyptians

The first peoples to leave a record of their experience with African blacks were the Egyptians. The history of Kushite-Egyptian contacts was in large part the story of Egypt's efforts to exploit the human and natural resources of Kush, and of Kush's response to the commercial and imperial ambitions of its northern neighbors. As early as the First Dynasty (ca. 3100–2890 B.C.) a raiding party of King Djer seems to have reached the Second Cataract.[1] Sneferu, the founder of the Fourth Dynasty (ca. 2613–2498 B.C.), made a sizable southern expedition in which he claimed the capture of 7,000 prisoners and 200,000 cattle.[2] Kushite resistance to Egyptian incursions into Nubia during the Old Kingdom is attested by an inscription from the tomb of Pepynakht, a noble from Elephantine (a city below the First Cataract), who reported that he had been commissioned by Pepy II in the Sixth Dynasty (ca. 2345–2181 B.C.) to pacify the countries of the south, that he had slain many leaders, and that he had returned with prisoners.[3] How many of Sneferu's captives were Negroid is not known, but Negroes of the pronounced type, as noted above, were among captives taken in the southern campaigns of Pepy I and II.[4] The troops, under the command of a general Uni (Weny) sent to Asia by Pepy I, included southern contingents,[5] and by around 2000 B.C. the Negro archers whose stelae have been mentioned earlier were apparently a sizable element in the population of Gebelein: a resident soldier boasts in his stele that he "surpassed the whole town in swiftness—its Nubians and Upper Egyptians."[6]

The opposition of Kushites to Egyptian undertakings in Nubia engaged the serious attention of the pharaohs of the Middle Kingdom (ca. 2133–1786 B.C.). One of Egypt's most impressive fortifications consisted of a chain of forts with massive walls, some thirty to forty feet high, in the area of the Second Cataract, many of which were constructed or extensively rebuilt by Sesostris III (ca. 1878–1843 B.C.).[7] A fear of the south was reflected in the so-called Execration Texts, two important series dating from the reign of Sesostris III and shortly thereafter, which included the names of some thirty Nubian peoples and Asiatic enemies considered actually or potentially dangerous.[8] Sesostris III was required to conduct several campaigns to the south, with the result that Nubia between the First and Second Cataracts became a possession of the pharaohs, except for a brief time during the Hyksos period, until the dissolution of the Empire. In a stele erected at Semna, about thirty-seven miles south of Wadi Halfa, Sesostris left no doubt about his determination to regulate traffic on the Nile: Semna was to be the point beyond which no southerner, except authorized merchants or emissaries, would be permitted to pass, by boat or land.[9]

An important key to Kushite strategy in resisting foreign exploitation was Nubia's promotion of its own interests at times when Egypt was experiencing internal military and political difficulties. During the late Second Intermediate Period (ca. 1786–1567 B.C.), peoples from Kerma, south of the Third Cataract, extended their influence to the north, and their rulers seem to have replaced the pharaohs as the controlling power of Lower Nubia and its trade. By the time of the Seventeenth Dynasty (ca. 1650–1567 B.C.) King Kamose frankly recognized the reality of Kushite power in Egypt in his statement that he shared the rule of Egypt with the Kushites and the Hyksos.[10] Apparently aware of the Kushite political and military position in Egypt, the Hyksos ruler Apophis sought the collaboration of the Kushites with this overture: "Come north. *Do not falter.* See he is here in my hand, and there is no one who is waiting for you in this (part of) Egypt. See I will not give him leave until you have arrived. Then we shall divide the towns of this Egypt and *our* [*two lands*] will be happy in joy."[11] The Kushite reply to this communication is not known because the message was intercepted by the Egyptians. Together with Kamose's straightforward assessment of southern power, however, the Hyksos invitation was a significant commentary on the role of the Kushite ruler in Egyptian politics of the time.

In their efforts to subdue a recalcitrant south, the first three pharaohs of the New Kingdom (1570–1085 B.C.) launched campaign after campaign. The result of this activity was that Kush from the First Cataract to Napata was conquered, administered as a province under a viceroy known as "the Royal Son of Kush," occupied for almost five hundred years, and required to pay an annual tribute and to provide manpower in support of Egypt's conquests and Asiatic wars. The reasons for Egypt's long-standing interest in Kush and its expectations from the south are illustrated by the tribute depicted in mural paintings from the tomb of Huy, the viceroy of Kush under Tutankhamun (1361–1352 B.C.). In one scene, servants from Upper Nubia bring tribute consisting only of raw materials, which include gold, semiprecious stones, leopard skins, cattle, and a giraffe. The tribute from Lower Nubia, though partially also in the form of raw materials, includes mostly goods such as bows, shields, and native arts and crafts.[12]

Although early in the Eighteenth Dynasty Tuthmosis I (1525–1512 B.C.) reported that he had decisively overthrown the Nubian chieftains, sporadic unrest continued to break out in Nubia, even toward the end of the New Kingdom.[13] Opinions differ as to the seriousness of the recorded rebellions. Pharaonic expeditions to the south, in the view of some scholars, were mere punitive police actions to quell local disturbances, but Vercoutter has noted that the ability of Kush to resist foreign domination has been underestimated by modern historians.[14] In spite of Kushite resistance, however, during the New Kingdom the control of the occupied south seems as a whole to have been relatively secure.

The Napatan and Meroïtic Kingdoms of Kush

One of the most intriguing facts of Nubian history was the ascendancy of the Napatan Kingdom of Kush (ca. 750–300 B.C.), after Nubia had been occupied by Egypt for almost five hundred years.[15] The meteoric rise of Napata was a remarkable achievement: in less than a hundred years the monarchy established itself, conquered Egypt, which it ruled as the Twenty-fifth Dynasty, and laid the foundations of a state that, with its later capital at Meroë (ca. 300 B.C.–350 A.D.), survived for more than a thousand years—a span longer than any single period of Egyptian unification.

It is relevant to raise the question of how a people coming from a region that had been under Egyptian domination for so long a period was able to conquer Egypt and to rule an empire that extended from the far south at Napata to the shores of the Mediterranean, some nine hundred miles as the crow flies. The emergence of the Napatans and their conquest of Egypt have often been explained as primarily a consequence of an Egypt weakened and divided by political disintegration. But the earlier history of Kush should not be overlooked. Several peoples from Lower and Upper Nubia had previously demonstrated their competence as soldiers and had acquired considerable knowledge of Egyptian politics. The Gebelein mercenaries probably participated in the conflicts of the First Intermediate Period (ca. 2181–2040 B.C.), which preceded the reunification of Egypt. Further, the Kushites of Kerma had been in contact with the Hyksos during the Second Intermediate Period, when Kamose's power was weakened in both the north and the south. Kushites had occupied high positions in Egyptian administration. One of the last viceroys of Kush in the New Kingdom was Pinehas, whose name suggests that he may have been black.[16] Even after the Egyptians had abandoned Nubia about 1085 B.C., Kushite troops continued to be active in Egyptian affairs. Zerah, described as a Kushite in the Old Testament and as the king of Ethiopia by Josephus, was, in the opinion of K. A. Kitchen, a general of Nubian extraction dispatched to Palestine about 897 B.C. by an aging Osorkon I.[17] In view of the long history of southern resistance to the Egyptians and of varied Nubian experience in Egypt and abroad, it is not surprising that peoples whose leaders had an obvious political savoir-faire and talent for military organization should succeed in turning the tables and vanquishing their former conquerors. In short, in a kind of Third Intermediate Period the Napatans outstripped their predecessors of an earlier intermediate period—the Kushites from Kerma—and this time seized control of Egypt up to the Mediterranean.

The Twenty-fifth Dynasty

Kashta, the first ruler of the Napatan Kingdom of Kush who is more than a shadowy figure, was able to seize control of Upper Egypt about 760 B.C. and to assume the title of pharaoh.[18] In an effective expedition to the north, Kashta's son and successor Piye (formerly read as Piankhy) overcame major opposition to Kushite rule in Egypt and defeated Tefnakht, a prince of the western Delta, who had played a key role in the northern resistance. An account of the Kushite campaign, recorded on a stele which Piye (ca. 747–716 B.C.) erected in the temple of Amun at Gebel Barkal, described the victorious Napatan as a capable military strategist, preferring surrender to bloodshed, scrupulously attentive to religious ritual, and respectful of Egyptian temples and gods.[19]

Shabaka (ca. 716–702 B.C.), Piye's brother and successor, consolidated earlier military gains, overcame scattered opposition in the north, and took effective control of Egypt up to the Asiatic border. The expansionist activity of Assyria involved the next Napatan King, Shebitku (ca. 702–690 B.C.), in the affairs of western Asia, where Sennacherib (705–681 B.C.), the Assyrian king, was confronted with resistance from Syria and Palestine in their struggle to remain independent of Assyria. Responding to an appeal from Hezekiah of Judah for assistance, Shebitku sent his younger brother Taharqa, in command of Egyptian-Nubian forces, into Asia, where Sennacherib defeated his Asiatic foes and Taharqa at Eltekeh in Palestine.

The power and influence of Taharqa (ca. 690–664 B.C.), Shebitku's successor, were considered a source of sufficient danger to Assyria's position in Palestine and Phoenicia to convince Esarhaddon, the king who succeeded Sennacherib, to invade Egypt. Though defeated by Taharqa in 674 B.C., Esarhaddon in a second invasion three years later destroyed Memphis, drove Taharqa to the south, returned to Asia with the Napatan's queen, heir apparent, and the booty he had plundered, and celebrated his victory by erecting triumphal monuments depicting a vanquished Negro and an Asiatic.[20] Esarhaddon's hope of crushing the Napatans decisively in Egypt, however, was not to be realized immediately; after the monarch's return to Assyria, both he and his successor, Ashurbanipal (669–626 B.C.), were confronted with further unrest in Egypt. Taharqa, with support from Delta chieftains and later his successor, Tanwetamani, undaunted by defeats at the hands of Ashurbanipal in Egypt, defied the Assyrians after their generals had returned to Asia, and succeeded in reestablishing Napatan rule for a time. Finally, though, Tanwetamani, after reoccupation of Egypt and short-lived success in the Delta, where his authority had been recognized, was defeated decisively by Ashurbanipal in 663 B.C. The Assyrians regained Memphis, sacked and plundered Thebes, and drove Tanwetamani apparently to Napata, marking the effective end of the rule of the Twenty-fifth Dynasty in Egypt.

Early Greek contacts with Napatan Ethiopians

The first European people to leave a record of their contacts with the Nubians of the Napatan and later the Meroïtic Kingdom of Kush were the Greeks, who originated the name Aithiopes (Ethiopians) for blacks.[21] The Napatans, although expelled from Egypt by the Assyrians in 663 B.C., still constituted a threat to the Egyptians. Psamtik II (594–588 B.C.) tried to eradicate memories of the Napatans by removing from the monuments of the Twenty-fifth Dynasty names of the Ethiopian pharaohs and replacing them with his own.[22] He considered it necessary to launch an expedition, which advanced into Nubia at least as far as the Second Cataract, but perhaps even farther.[23] The Greeks who served in Psamtik's army were among the first Europeans to confront blacks face to face in Africa. While campaigning in Nubia, Greek mercenaries certainly became acquainted with the reason for Psamtik's southern mission—to thwart the military plans of the Napatans and to prevent a resurgence of Napatan dominion in Egypt. Upon their return to Greece, mercenaries doubtlessly related to friends what they had seen and heard about the history of the Ethiopians, once rulers of Egypt. It is highly probable that descriptions of Ethiopians circulated by mercenaries such as the Colophonian Pabis, one of the Greeks whose names are known from graffiti scratched on a colossal statue at Abu Simbel, account for the fact that Xenophanes of Colophon was the first Greek writer to designate an Ethiopian by a physical characteristic other than color.[24] The prominence given to Negro warriors in sixth-century vase paintings may likewise echo reports of Ethiopian military repute and may reflect Greek experience in Egypt.[25]

Ethiopians in the civilian or military employ of the Egyptian ruler Amasis (ca. 569–525 B.C.) during his occupation of Cyprus increased Greek awareness of blacks in the sixth century.[26] A delegation from Elis is reported to have been sent to Africa in the Twenty-sixth Dynasty to seek the advice of Egyptians on the rules governing the Olympic Games.[27] Continued relations between Egypt and Elis may explain the presence of Ethiopians in Greece suggested by Aristotle's comments on racial mixture in the family of a woman from Elis, who was the mother of a child by an Ethiopian.[28] By the sixth century B.C. Greeks had been firmly established in Naukratis, where the Negroes of Greek artists attest a firsthand acquaintance with Ethiopians. Travelers to Egypt and Ethiopia furthered knowledge of Ethiopians among the Greeks. Herodotus, whose history includes the first detailed extant account of Ethiopia and Ethiopians, traveled as far south as Elephantine.[29] Simonides the Younger, one of several reported visitors to Ethiopia, is said to have lived for five years in Meroë in preparation for a book on the region.[30] The presence of Ethiopian mercenaries in the army of Xerxes during his campaign of 480–479 B.C. enabled mainland Greeks to see Ethiopians in person for the first time in rather large numbers.[31] The popularity of Negroes in the art of the fifth century and of Ethiopian themes in the theater was probably a reflection of an interest stimulated both by the experience of Greek residents in Egypt and contemporary reports of Ethiopian soldiers.[32]

Meroïtic Ethiopians and the Greco-Roman World

Some Greeks had acquired a firsthand knowledge of Ethiopians from the Napatan Kingdom of Kush; others had received reports of the Ethiopian Dynasty from travelers in Egypt or from the history of Herodotus.[33] It was, however, primarily the Meroïtic Ethiopians who at various times from about 300 B.C. to 350 A.D. evoked the attention of classical writers and attracted visitors to Nubia.

Unlike the Napatans, the Meroïtes made no serious attempt to conquer and rule Egypt; they concentrated instead on maintaining the independence of Nubia. This policy in general proved to be successful, with the result that the Meroïtes were able to create substantial obstacles to the furtherance of Ptolemaic and Roman plans for the military occupation and commercial exploitation of Nubia. For a considerable time the Meroïtic state enjoyed an active mercantile economy, and during the first century before and after Christ developed a greater volume of trade and a material prosperity more broadly based than previously.[34] Between the period of the Napatan dominion of Egypt in the latter part of the eighth century B.C. and the collapse of the Meroïtic kingdom in the early fourth century A.D., approximately a thousand years elapsed. The history of Meroë, as P. L. Shinnie has observed, "stands as a major landmark of ancient Africa ... an African civilization, firmly based on African soil, and developed by an African population."[35]

Meroïtes and the Ptolemies

Nubia's natural resources were as attractive to the Ptolemies as they had been to the Egyptians. The Ptolemies were particularly interested in access to gold mines in the Nubian and eastern deserts, and in the acquisition of elephants for military purposes.[36] The Nubian activity of the second Ptolemy (Philadelphus, 283–246 B.C.) illustrates the kind of interest the Ptolemies were to have in the south.[37] Philadelphus seized a portion of the country of the "black Ethiopians," conducted elephant-hunting expeditions, and organized a great procession in Alexandria that paraded elephants and Ethiopians carrying tusks of ivory, ebony logs, and vessels of gold and silver.[38]

Ethiopians are reported to have resisted Ptolemaic commercial and military policy in Nubia. At times they besieged Ptolemaic positions;[39] at other times they allied themselves with Egyptian insurgents. In some of the Egyptian rebellions that plagued the later Ptolemies, Ethiopians played a role.[40] It is not unlikely that respect for the courage and reputation of Ethiopian warriors[41] gave rise to a Ptolemaic policy of recruiting southern mercenaries. Because of their experience and skill in handling elephants, Ethiopians were probably employed by the Ptolemies as elephant trainers and mahouts.[42] Furthermore, the existence of amicable relations with some Meroïtes at the end of the third century B.C. is suggested by the building programs of Meroïtic rulers at Philae, a border area under Ptolemaic control.

Knowledge of Ethiopia and Ethiopians was considerably enlarged during the Ptolemaic era, beginning at least with the reign of Philadelphus. In a list of visitors to Ethiopia, Pliny includes Timosthenes, a commander of the navy of Philadelphus, reported to have traveled from Syene to Meroë, and a certain Dalion said to have been the first Greek to penetrate Ethiopia beyond Meroë.[43] The navigator Eudoxus of Cyzicus, who lived in the second century B.C., is reported to have noted similarities in the language spoken by the inhabitants along the coasts of east and west Africa.[44] Of the extant Ptolemaic treatises concerning Ethiopia, the most detailed information is found in the *De Mari Erythraeo* of Agatharchides, one of the major sources used by Diodorus, who himself had talked with Ethiopian ambassadors living in Egypt. Such works point to a considerable contemporary interest in up-to-date accounts of the people and country of blacks who, as Hellenistic art attests, were a familiar sight in Egypt.

Rome and Meroïtic Ethiopians

During their occupation of Egypt from the Augustan era to the sixth century A.D., the Romans found Nubian opposition a threat to their southern boundary. Like the Egyptians and Ptolemies before them, the Romans were required to evolve a policy to secure their southern boundary and to protect Nilotic trade routes.[45] Cornelius Gallus, the first prefect of Egypt, was faced with rebellions in the Theban

area, which he easily crushed. With the aim of regulating the southern frontier, Gallus advanced beyond the First Cataract, a region
that, according to the extravagant claim he made in an inscription
of 29 B.C., had never been penetrated by the armies of the Roman
peoples or the kings of Egypt. In a meeting with Ethiopian ambassadors at Philae, Gallus effected an arrangement whereby the Ethiopian king was admitted to the protection of Rome, and the Triakontaschoinos, an area of the Nile Valley north of the Second Cataract,
was to be governed by a subordinate ruler (tyrannus). The inade-
quacy of this policy of a buffer state became apparent a few years
later when Aelius Gallus, the successor of Cornelius Gallus, had left
Egypt with a large Roman force for an expedition to Arabia. During
his absence the Meroïtes, apparently well posted by their intelli-
gence officers on the condition of Roman forces remaining in Egypt,
crossed the Roman frontiers, captured several towns, including Elephantine and Philae, defeated three Roman cohorts stationed there,
enslaved the inhabitants, and seized the statues of Augustus. The
several countermeasures of C. Petronius, the next prefect, according
to Strabo, resulted in the capture and destruction of Napata, the enslavement of its inhabitants, and the sale of prisoners (fig. 29a-b), a
thousand of whom were sent to Augustus.[46] The extremely favorable terms of the peace that Augustus granted the Ethiopian ambassadors at Samos suggest that Strabo was exaggerating the
Roman victory. The emperor granted the envoys of the Ethiopian
queen (fig. 30) everything they pleaded for, including remission of
the tribute Augustus had imposed.[47] Or perhaps, as Shelagh Jameson has assessed this Roman encounter with Ethiopians, the ancient
sources "smack of apologia: Augustus was aiming at territorial expansion and failed."[48]

The concessions Augustus made to the Ethiopians and his policy
of accommodation were apparently in Rome's interests, for little is
heard of Roman activity in Ethiopia until the third century. Two
major reasons appear in the ancient sources for Nero's dispatch of
praetorian troops to Ethiopia—reconnoitering for a campaign and
exploration of the sources of the Nile.[49] The peaceful Ethiopian-
Roman relations of the first centuries after Christ, interrupted only
by an occasional military engagement, such as that in the second
century A.D. between a Roman cavalry unit and the Ethiopians,[50]

undoubtedly owed not a little to Augustus' foresight and to the diplomatic negotiations of Ethiopian and Roman ambassadors, some of
whose names appear in inscriptions dating from 13 B.C. and later.[51]
Trade flourished, the Romans exchanging luxury goods for the coveted products of Nilotic trade and animals for gladiatorial games.

At various times from the middle of the third century to late in
the sixth century, the Romans experienced serious trouble from another southern people—the Blemmyes, described variously as a
black-skinned Ethiopian race, burnt-colored and woolly-haired, a
people identified by nearly all modern scholars with today's Beja
tribes from the Red Sea hills.[52] During this period the Blemmyes attacked settlements in the vicinity of the Roman frontier, participated
in Egyptian rebellions, and raided Christian communities.[53] An indication of the seriousness of this situation is reflected in the arrangement Diocletian made toward the close of the third century.
Abandoning Lower Nubia, the emperor withdrew the Roman frontier to the First Cataract; settled another people, the Nobatae, as
buffers between the Blemmyes and the new Roman boundary;
promised an annual tribute to both the Blemmyes and Nobatae,
which they were still receiving more than two hundred years later;
and, with the hope that the experience of common worship would
result in friendship with Rome's southern neighbors, settled priests
from among Romans, Blemmyes, and Nobatae at certain temples
and altars.[54]

Romans and Ethiopians in Northwest Africa

A majority of Ethiopians known to the Greeks and Romans were
blacks from the Nile Valley. But Roman contacts with Ethiopians
from northwest Africa probably began with the Punic Wars and
continued from time to time during the Roman occupation of
Africa. If the usual interpretation of the Negroes and elephants appearing on a third-century B.C. coinage (fig. 31a-b) is correct, Romans
encountered blacks of the pronounced Negroid type as mahouts in
the Carthaginian army. One view holds that the coins were issued
after the defeat of the Carthaginians at Panormus in 250 B.C. when
L. Caecilius Metellus captured a large number of elephants; others
associate the coinage with Hannibal and the impression the gen-

eral's Negro mahouts made upon the population of northern Italy.[55] Also worthy of note in this connection is Plautus' mention of blacks, suggesting the presence of blacks on Italian soil.[56] At any rate, whatever the precise meaning of the coinage, an early impression of Ethiopians in Italy was that of Ethiopian mahouts—an image perpetuated by several literary references to Ethiopian skill in handling elephants, by Arrian's statement that Ethiopian and Indian armies used elephants for military purposes before the Macedonians and the Carthaginians, and perhaps by reports of the importance of elephants in the life of Meroïtes.[57]

Subsequent Roman experience in northwest Africa resulted in further contacts with black warriors. Among these were the Garamantes, an Ethiopian or mixed black-white people,[58] described as "an indomitable tribe and one always engaged in brigandage on their neighbors."[59] Their anti-Roman activity, for example, required L. Cornelius Balbus, proconsul of Africa (21–20 B.C.?), to launch a punitive and deterrent campaign in which Garama, their capital, was captured.[60] The Garamantes gave their support to Tacfarinas, a Numidian, who stirred up a serious insurrection in 17 A.D., but, upon the defeat of Tacfarinas, they dispatched envoys to Rome where, Tacitus reports, they were "a rare spectacle."[61] In spite of a plea to the Romans that their offenses be pardoned, the Garamantes later gave assistance to the Oeans during a civil war between Lepcis and Oea.[62] Reports of two Roman expeditions into the interior of northwest Africa are recorded: one was led by Septimius Flaccus, probably the propraetorial legate of Numidia, who advanced sometime after 76 A.D. a distance of "three months" beyond the country of the Garamantes; the other was under the leadership of Julius Maternus who, accompanied by the king of the Garamantes perhaps between 83 and 92 A.D., made a joint march toward Ethiopian territory, reaching "Agisymba."[63] Whatever the precise purpose of the missions, these encounters with Ethiopians provided additional substance for the Roman view of blacks as warriors and enemies of Rome.

Blacks participated in the revolts that broke out sporadically during the Roman occupation of northwest Africa. The herms of a Negro and a white (a Libyan), perhaps part of a triumphal monument, found in the baths of Antoninus Pius at Carthage (fig. 32a,b,c), have been interpreted as representative of the natives who opposed the Roman presence in Africa.[64] Numerous Ethiopian auxiliaries, according to Ammianus Marcellinus, were recruited by Firmus, the Moorish chieftain, who raised a revolt in 372 A.D.[65] Corippus' catalogue of native chieftains killed in Moorish rebellions toward the middle of the sixth century included blacks.[66] Roman military units enrolled black soldiers from northwest Africa, continuing a Mediterranean practice of employing black troops dating back to pharaonic times. An Ethiopian was reported among the auxiliaries of Septimius Severus in Britain, perhaps part of the *numerus Maurorum*, billeted at Aballava (Burgh-by-Sands), one of the forts astride Hadrian's Wall.[67] A scene on an early third-century sarcophagus (fig. 33) shows, to the right of a general whose features resemble those of Septimius Severus, three soldiers receiving suppliant Roman captives. One of these soldiers is a Negro, as is also perhaps at least one of those on the Arch of Septimius Severus in the Roman Forum—not unexpected in view of the emperor's African origins.[68] The exact racial composition of Rome's elite mobile Moorish cavalry commanded by Lusius Quietus is not known. But the fact that the Moorish horsemen on the column of Trajan are depicted with curly hair may be the sculptor's method of indicating Negroid admixture.[69] And it should be recalled that Lusius Quietus himself, in the opinion of some scholars, was Negroid, an Ethiopian from Cerne, perhaps Mogador Island, off the Atlantic coast of Morocco.[70]

This brief look at the intermingling of blacks and Mediterranean whites has shown the importance of commercial and political interests and the role of military engagements in the development of such encounters. Also notable is the recurrent, and at times substantial, resistance of Nubian populations to foreign intervention in their country, and the often prominent position of Nubians in the politics of the times.

Another point emerging from this survey is the fact that, beginning with the pharaonic period, involvement in military engagements of various kinds provided a major avenue by which blacks found their way to many parts of the ancient world—a means of dispersal of blacks deserving more attention than it has received. Whether fighting in the interest of Nubia or as auxiliaries of other peoples, captured blacks were enslaved like other prisoners of war in antiquity, and, in view of the wide range of military engagements in which they were involved, it is reasonable to suppose that captives were a chief source of black slaves. It is often difficult, however, to determine whether blacks mentioned in ancient texts were prisoners of war or acquired through slave trade.[71] The few references to blacks specifically designated as slaves rarely reveal their origin or the method of acquisition. Our sources seldom provide even as much information as Suetonius did in his life of Terence. Although the biographer mentions the poet's color (*colore fusco*) and place of birth (Carthage), he adds only the reasons for his doubts that Terence had been a prisoner of war.[72] Some black warriors who escaped capture probably settled in areas of the countries where they had fought, and others, attracted by what they had seen during their campaigns, returned later, in a spirit of adventure or in the pursuit of economic gain. A failure to relate the Kushites and Ethiopians of texts and inscriptions and the blacks of artists to the long history of meetings between blacks and Mediterranean whites outlined here has often given rise to a distorted image of blacks in antiquity.

3

IMAGES
AND
ATTITUDES

Approximately three thousand years elapsed between the first Egyptian and the last classical records of blacks. In spite of differences in outlook—from the heavy military emphasis of Egyptian and Assyrian documents to the more comprehensive Greco-Roman view—the image of Nubia and Nubians from the Pharaohs to the Caesars was in significant respects remarkably similar and consistent.

The Egyptian View

Early in their intervention in Nubia, the Egyptians encountered Kushite opposition. How did the Egyptians react to the peoples who resisted their policy of aggression with varying degrees of success and eventually conquered Egypt itself? On this point early Egyptian documents report little more than the names of southerners encountered, numbers of captives, and items of booty. As contacts with the south increased, however, official accounts of Nubian campaigns are more revealing. Nubia came to be referred to as *Kush-Khesyt*, formerly read as "Kush the Contemptible" but now as "Kush the Defeated."[1] Sesostris III (ca. 1878–1843 B.C.) characterized the Kushites as "craven," "poor and broken in heart," and "not a people of might."[2] These descriptions of Egypt's southern foes apparently overstated the pharaoh's case, as he himself suggested by his emphasis on the importance of the future maintenance of the southern boundary he had established at Semna: "Now, as for every son of mine who shall maintain this boundary, which my majesty has made, he is my son ... Now, as for him who shall relax it, and shall not fight for it; he is not my son, he is not born to me."[3] Further, Sesostris' impressive fortifications, the Execration Texts dating from his reign, and subsequent events, especially in the Second Intermediate Period, are evidence that the Kushites constituted a greater danger than that implied by the contemptuous language of Sesostris' inscriptions.

In the Second Intermediate Period toward the end of the Seventeenth Dynasty (ca. 1650–1567 B.C.) Kamose spoke out candidly about Kushite power in his day: "Let me understand what this strength of mine is for! (One) prince [the Hyksos] is in Avaris, another is in Ethiopia, and (here) I sit associated with an Asiatic and a Negro! Each man has his slice of this Egypt, dividing the land with me."[4] Tuthmosis I (ca. 1525–1512 B.C.), on the other hand, early in the New Kingdom reported that he had overthrown the chiefs of the Nubians, described his enemies as "helpless, defenseless in his grasp," and boasted that there was not "a single survivor among them."[5] But the Kushite uprisings and disturbances that occurred even in the last dynasty of the New Kingdom suggest that Tuthmosis, like Sesostris III earlier, was exaggerating and that the official language of his inscriptions was not to be taken literally.

Frequently contrasted with Asiatics, Egypt's southern enemies figured much more prominently in the art of the New Kingdom than before. A protome in the form of a lion's head in Egyptian blue, now in the Norbert Schimmel Collection, perhaps originally one of a set of nine designating Egypt's traditional enemies (fig. 34), holds a thick-lipped, open-mouthed, prognathous black in its gaping jaws.[6] Dating from the reign of Amenophis III (1417–1379 B.C.), it is one of the finest examples of the lion motif, a symbol that the pharaohs used to dramatize their ability to attack their foes without warning and to control them. A wooden chest of Tutankhamun (1361–1352 B.C.) shows, in an extraordinary miniature technique, the king slaughtering Syrians on one side and blacks in a corresponding scene on the other side.[7] This black-white contrast is highlighted also in other objects from the reign of Tutankhamun: a footstool in wood with overlay of blue glass and gilt stucco, decorated with alternating Kushite and Asiatic captives (fig. 35); and a ceremonial throwing stick that attractively combines a Negro in ebony and a bearded white in ivory.[8] Splendid examples of Egypt's enemies from the reign of Ramesses III (1198–1166 B.C.), in the form of brilliantly glazed tiles from a temple at Medinet Habu (fig. 36), portray vividly the racial features and national dress of Negroes and Asiatics.[9] The many representatives of Negroes as enemies in art of the

New Kingdom, when considered in the light of Kushite might and resistance throughout Egypt's history, suggest that the portrayals, though in part "magical," "propagandistic," or "contemptuous," stemmed also from a deep-seated fear of Kushites rooted in reality.[10] Kush, as the Twenty-fifth Dynasty was to prove, was a potential threat to the stability of the Egyptian empire.

Worthy of note is the fact that, despite Egypt's difficulties with its southern foes, the *Great Hymn to the Aten* looks objectively at mankind's diversity in skin color, speech, and character, making no claim to Egyptian superiority. Seeing all peoples as creations of the Aten, the sun disk, the unknown author, often identified as Akhenaten (1379–1362 B.C.), predates the north-south contrast of the Greco-Roman environment theory.[11]

> O sole god, like whom there is no other!
> Thou didst create the world according to thy desire,
> . . .
> The countries of Syria and Nubia, the land of Egypt,
> Thou settest every man in his place . . .
> Their tongues are separate in speech,
> And their natures as well;
> Their skins are distinguished,
> As thou distinguishest the foreign peoples.[12]

Several forces tended to lessen acrimony and to foster amicable relationships between Egyptians and Kushites. An obvious illustration of this side of the coin was the longstanding Egyptian practice of employing military contingents from the south. Blacks, like other foreigners, played an increasingly important role in the Egyptian army of the New Kingdom and contributed to Egypt's success during the expansion of its empire. Not all Kushite mercenaries in the Egyptian army were inducted by force: volunteers saw the advantages of a career in the Egyptian army—an avenue to prestige in Egypt. The cooperation of Kushites with the enemy may seem inconsistent with loyalty to homeland, but it should be kept in mind that Kushite auxiliaries did not owe allegiance to Nubia as a whole and that they doubtless were not expected to attack their own districts. Further, the depressed conditions of areas of Nubia ravaged by the occupying Egyptian army and the prospect of benefits from a military career were important factors in the decision of Kushite mercenaries.[13]

Close ties and bonds of genuine friendship, dating back at least to the period of the Gebelein mercenaries, probably developed between Egyptians and the black warriors whom they came to know at home and abroad. A relief of the late Eighteenth or early Nineteenth Dynasty from Sesebi shows two Nubian archers of monumental size, one supporting the other (fig. 37). A figure on the right, holding his arm around the neck of his companion, has apparently been wounded and is being assisted by his comrade-in-arms. This memorial, in the opinion of Elizabeth Riefstahl, gives the impression of "compassion and shared suffering."[14] To the courage of soldiers like those depicted in this relief some Egyptians no doubt owed their lives. In short, black soldiers helped Egypt to defend itself at home and abroad. It is likely that many Kushites gained respect, if not gratitude, for their contribution to the military efforts of the pharaohs.

In spite of the ups and downs in Kushite-Egyptian relations, intermarriages between Egyptians and women from the south were not uncommon, and Nubian ladies were found in the harems of the pharaohs. As early as the Fourth Dynasty, we have seen, a noble of the court of Memphis had a Negro wife, whose position in the court was equal to that of Egyptian women.[15] In commenting on the women in the household of Mentuhotpe II (ca. 2060–2010 B.C.), H. E. Winlock has called attention to the Nubian features of the tatooed dancing girls of the pharaoh's reign, to the rich brown complexion of Ashayet, a queen in his harem, and to the ebony black color of her companion, Kemsit. The fondness of this pharaoh and his nobles for southern women, in Winlock's opinion, accounts for more than a "trace of the brunette complexion in the Theban aristocracy of 4,000 years ago."[16] The mother of Amenemhet I (1991–1962 B.C.) was a woman of the land of Nubia.[17] The features and color of Queen Tiy, the influential consort of Amenophis III (fig. 38), point to Nubian extraction.[18] Black warriors had for centuries constituted an element in the population of Egypt. As the number of these soldiers increased during the Middle Kingdom, there is little doubt that, like the earlier Gebelein mercenaries, some married Egyptian women. Ties of blood and kinship, therefore, introduced a factor that would have tended to influence Egyptian attitudes toward Kushites.

The Twenty-fifth Dynasty was a new experience for Egyptians: the victors had been vanquished. How were the Napatan conquerors perceived by Egyptians? How did the Napatans, after experiencing years of Egyptian exploitation and occupation, react to their former lords? The Napatans of the Twenty-fifth Dynasty appeared to Egyptians in many respects as native rulers rather than as foreign invaders. No strangers to Egyptian culture, numbers of Kushites had been absorbed into the Egyptian army, some occupying high rank in provincial administrations. In the New Kingdom sons of the Kushite nobility had been educated at the Egyptian court, together with the sons of Asiatic nobility, as part of an Egyptian policy of assimilation. Adopting traditional pharaonic titles such as "Lord of the Two Lands" and "Beloved of Amun," the rulers of the Twenty-fifth Dynasty continued the image of the ancient pharaohs. Piye's attention to religious ritual and respect for Egyptian temples and gods[19] adumbrated the religious interest of later Napatan kings. Apparently regarding themselves as defenders and perpetuators of Egyptian culture, the victorious southern rulers initiated a new era of building by renovating and enlarging existing temples and by new construction in various parts of Egypt, especially the Theban region.[20] Upon the instructions of Shabaka, a theological text dating from the Old Kingdom was recopied on stone to replace a worm-eaten original.[21] The so-called Saite renaissance in Egyptian art had its beginning in the Twenty-fifth Dynasty and can be attributed, according to W. S. Smith, to the new strength imparted to the country by the Kushite conquerors.[22] For several decades under the Ethiopian Dynasty Egypt also enjoyed an improved economic situation. It was not surprising, therefore, that some Delta chieftains looked to Kushite leadership in efforts to cast off the yoke of Assyrian domination of Egypt, which they had found more oppressive than Napatan rule. Turning to Taharqa as one of their own, rebellious Egyptians, according to the Assyrian king Ashurbanipal (669–626 B.C.), sought the Napatan king's assistance in freeing Egypt from Assyrian dominion with this plea: "Let there be peace between us and let us come to mutual understanding; we will divide the country between us, no foreigner shall be ruler among us!"[23] In other words, Taharqa was a native son, not a foreign invader like the Assyrians.

Nubia appears in some sources as a region offering sympathetic asylum to refugees and lending a friendly ear to numerous causes. An otherwise unidentified "Amenophis," while preparing to confront his enemies, took refuge in Ethiopia, where his son had been apparently sent for safekeeping. The Ethiopian king at the time, according to Manetho, not only welcomed Amenophis and his huge following but provided them with food and stationed Ethiopian troops on the Egyptian frontier to protect the Egyptian king and his subjects.[24]

In the period immediately following the rule of the Ethiopian Dynasty, Egyptian warriors of Psamtik I (ca. 663–609 B.C.) were dissatisfied, according to Herodotus, with conditions in their garrison, defected from Elephantine to Ethiopia, settled south of Meroë on land they received as a gift from the Ethiopian king, and apparently married Ethiopian women.[25] Herodotus' account is another illustration of the kind of information circulated concerning relationships between Egyptians and Kushites that existed before and after the Twenty-fifth Dynasty. Strabo's discussion of population movements refers to migrations of Egyptians into Ethiopia as if they were well known.[26] As late as the Thirtieth Dynasty Nectanebo II (359–341 B.C.), the last of the native pharaohs, in order to prevent a second Persian conquest is reported to have fled to Ethiopia, with the expectation of receiving assistance. That Alexander the Great was considering a campaign into Ethiopia was, in the opinion of R. Lane Fox, much more than a rumor because Nectanebo was believed ready to return from Ethiopia, where he had support, and to reestablish his rule.[27]

Such accounts, even if apocryphal or inaccurate as to details, project an image of Nubia as a haven of refuge for Egyptians. An important factor inspiring some of the Egyptian rebellions that plagued the later Ptolemies was perhaps the maintenance of a continued pharaonic tradition in the south, which, unlike Egypt, had not been subjugated by the Ptolemies. The existence of an independent Nubia just beyond their southern frontier was a source of hope to Egyptian nationalists: memories of a sympathetic Kush, source of asylum and assistance in the past, could not be easily eradicated.

Kushites as Seen by the Assyrians

Assyrian annals relating to the Kushites deal largely with Nubian-Assyrian military encounters and with Napatan politics of the Twenty-fifth Dynasty, which jeopardized Assyria's position in the Near East. In Assyrian art, we have seen, Assyria's Egyptian enemy was the Negro. A similar view is recorded in Assyrian royal documents that reflect the respect won by the Napatan military in Asia. An inscription of King Sennacherib refers to the aid that Hezekiah and the people of Judah had received from the Twenty-fifth Dynasty: "[They] had become afraid and had called (for help) upon the kings of Egypt (and) the bowmen, the chariot-(corps) and the cavalry of the king of Ethiopia ... an enemy beyond counting—and they (actually) had come to their assistance."[28] Sennacherib, the inscription continues, defeated them at Eltekeh and personally captured alive the charioteers of the combined Egyptian-Napatan forces. Baal, king of Tyre, apparently also looked to the Napatans for support. Esarhaddon, Sennacherib's successor, recorded that Baal had "put his trust upon his friend Tirhakah ... king of Nubia, and therefore had thrown off the yoke of Ashur ... answering [my admonitions] with insolence."[29] With the hope of preventing further Napatan intervention in Asian affairs, Esarhaddon decided upon an Egyptian campaign. His account of the siege and destruction of Memphis suggests that his success was not easily won. The symbolic victory stelae depicting an Asian and a Negro that Esarhaddon erected upon his return to Asia "accorded rather with the wishes of the Assyrian king than with the facts. Ba'alu rejected his terms, and Tarku was still master of his native land, Kush."[30]

Ashurbanipal, who succeeded Esarhaddon, acknowledged that he had to cover much of the same ground against the Napatans as his predecessor: "I marched against Egypt ... and Ethiopia ... Tirhakah ..., king of Egypt ... and Nubia ..., whom Esarhaddon, king of Assyria, my own father, had defeated and in whose country he (Esarhaddon) had ruled ... forgot the might of Ashur ... He turned against the kings (and) regents whom my own father had appointed in Egypt. He entered and took residence in Memphis ... the city which my own father had conquered and incorporated into Assyrian territory."[31] Ashurbanipal continues his account by stating that he reinstalled his father's regents who had fled in the face of Taharqa's uprising, seized control of Egypt and Nubia again, strengthened the Assyrian garrisons, and made regulations more firm. But the monarch was to learn that, after his victorious return to Nineveh, his appointees in the Delta had broken their oaths and called upon Taharqa to return to Egypt and join them in rebellion against Assyria. In the end, though, the superior Assyrian military forces won the day and ended Napatan supremacy in Egypt. The wisdom of the Napatan decision to retreat to Nubia after Ashur-banipal's sack of Thebes in 663 B.C., however, might be seen in the fact that the Assyrian empire collapsed at the end of the seventh century B.C., but the independent Kingdom of Kush, with its later capital at Meroë, lasted until about 350 A.D.

Kushites in the Old Testament

The image of Kushites in the Old Testament provides an additional view of Nubia and Nubians as seen by another Eastern people. In the Old Testament Kush appears as an independent country, economically and politically important, extending from Syene far to the south of Egypt, one of the geographical extremes of the world.[32] Its inhabitants were tall and smooth-skinned;[33] their blackness was proverbial.[34] Kushite ambassadors traveled along the Nile in vessels of reed.[35] Moses married a Kushite woman and when, Aaron and Miriam rebuked Moses for this, "the anger of the Lord was roused against them, and he left them; and ... there was Miriam, her skin diseased and white as snow."[36] A Kushite, apparently a trusted messenger, carried the report of Absalom's defeat and death from Joab to David.[37] Ebed-melech, a Kushite eunuch in the palace of Zedekiah, upon hearing of Jeremiah's imprisonment and impending death from starvation, interceded with Zedekiah on the prophet's behalf and helped ease Jeremiah's pain as he was lifted from a pit. The Lord was pleased with Ebed-melech and revealed through Jeremiah that the eunuch would survive the destruction of Jerusalem: "Go and say to Ebed-melech the Cushite ... I will preserve you on that day ... and you shall not fall a victim to the sword; because you trusted in me."[38]

Kush appears conspicuously in the Old Testament as one of the great military nations of the time. A distant and powerful people in the extreme south, the Kushites are contrasted with the Assyrians in the far north. According to Chronicles, Shishak (Shoshenq), king of Egypt, with innumerable troops including Kushites, captured the fortified cities of Judah, reached Jerusalem, and removed the treasures of the house of the Lord.[39] Though "dreaded near and far, a nation strong and proud,"[40] like other peoples the Kushites experienced defeat as well. When Zerah the Kushite came "with an army a million strong and three hundred chariots," the Lord answered the prayer of Asa, king of Judah, and gave victory to Asa. The Kushites were broken, many fell, and Judah carried off much booty.[41] Upon hearing that Taharqa was on his way to help Hezekiah, King Sennacherib taunted Hezekiah for having faith in the Kushites, since it was well known that other nations had been exterminated by Assyria's superior skill and numbers.[42] Judah should not place confidence in the pharaoh of Egypt, Sennacherib warned, because "Egypt is a splintered cane that will run into a man's hand and pierce it if he leans on it."[43] Sennacherib's boast turned out to be partially true with respect to Kush; the Assyrians succeeded in bringing an end to Kushite supremacy in Egypt, but Kush remained an independent kingdom. Even decades after Ashurbanipal had sacked Thebes and driven Tanwetamani back to Napata, the memory of Kush's former power was still alive: the prophet Nahum recalled that "Cush and Egypt were her [Thebes] strength, and it was boundless."[44]

Like other nations, Kush was subject to God's judgment. God said to Ezekiel that at the day of reckoning "a sword will come upon Egypt, and there will be anguish in Cush."[45] The conversion of the Kushites was prefigured: "From beyond the rivers of Cush," said the prophet Zephaniah, "my suppliants of the Dispersion shall bring me tribute."[46] "Let Nubia stretch out her hands to God," reads a verse from Psalms.[47] And Kush was to be among the nations to acknowledge Zion as a spiritual home: "I will count Egypt and Babylon among my friends; Philistine, Tyrian and Nubian shall be there; and Zion shall be called a mother in whom men of every race are born."[48] In short, in the Old Testament Kushites were looked upon as one in a family of nations, a people whose color in the eyes of both God and Moses was of no moment—ideas that were to figure prominently in the early Christian view of blacks.

The Image of Ethiopians in the Greco-Roman World

In their observations on Ethiopia and Ethiopians, classical writers provided a much more detailed and variegated picture of Nubians than any other Mediterranean peoples. Not limiting their interest primarily to military coverage, the Greeks and Romans in their accounts of the Ethiopians touched on a broad range of subjects, including anthropology, sociology, history, mythology, and religion.

From Homer to the fifth century

Ethiopians appear for the first time in Greek literature in the Homeric poems, where they are remote peoples, the most distant of men, sundered in twain, dwelling by the streams of Ocean, some where the sun rises, some where it sets. Their only earthly visitor was Menelaus, who said that he came to their country after wanderings in Cyprus, Phoenicia, and Egypt. Homer's Olympian gods were fond of visiting the "blameless" Ethiopians: Zeus, followed by all the other gods, feasted for twelve days with them; Poseidon and Iris shared their sacrifices.[49] Epaphus, according to Hesiod, was the child of the almighty son of Kronos, and from him sprang the black Libyans and high-souled Ethiopians.[50] These early Ethiopians are shadowy individuals; their ethnic identity and precise location, uncertain. By the time of Xenophanes, however, word had reached the Greeks that Ethiopians were black-faced and flat-nosed[51] and, by the fifth century, that they lived in Africa south of Egypt.

The first writer to enlarge upon Homer's blameless and Xenophanes' flat-nosed Ethiopians was Herodotus. African Ethiopians, according to Herodotus, differed from the Ethiopians of the east only in speech and hair, the former being the most woolly-haired people on earth and the latter having straight hair.[52] The capital of African Ethiopia was Meroë, a "great city" whose inhabitants greatly honored the gods Zeus (Amun) and Dionysus (Osiris).[53] Ethiopia, according to Herodotus, had been ruled by only one Egyptian king, though it had contributed eighteen kings as rulers of Egypt.[54] One of these was Sabacos, who invaded Egypt with a great army of Ethiopians and ruled Egypt for fifty years. As king of Egypt, Sabacos never put wrongdoers to death but instead required them, according to the severity of their offense, to contribute to civic improvement by raising the embankments of their cities. Uneasy lest he commit sacrilege, Sabacos voluntarily retired from Egypt after he had been terrified by a dream that he would assemble Egyptian priests and put them to death.[55]

Like Sabacos, the king of the Macrobian Ethiopians, called the tallest and most handsome men on earth,[56] had a high regard for justice. Having discerned the deception of the spies whom the Persian king Cambyses (ca. 530–522 B.C.) had sent when planning an Ethiopian expedition, the perspicacious Macrobian king remarked that the Persian king was unjust, for no just man would covet a land not his own. And, with a dramatic display of his dexterity in handling a huge bow, he instructed Cambyses' spies to inform the king that "when the Persians can draw a bow of this greatness as easily as I do, then to bring overwhelming odds to attack the Macrobian Ethiopians; but till then, to thank the gods who put it not in the minds of the sons of the Ethiopians to win more territory than they have."[57] Herodotus continues that Cambyses, receiving this response, became angry and, acting like a mad man, embarked without adequate preparation upon an Ethiopian campaign, which he was forced to abandon because of a shortage of supplies and cannibalism among his troops.[58] Further, Cambyses imposed no tribute on either the Ethiopians bordering Egypt whom he had subdued on his ill-fated march to the Macrobians or on those living near Nysa. These Ethiopians, according to Herodotus, brought gifts to the Persians every other year—about two quarts of gold, two hundred blocks of ebony, five boys, and twenty large elephant tusks.[59] A striking confirmation of this statement appears in a scene on a relief of the Audience Hall at Persepolis begun by Darius: among the gifts brought by a diplomatic delegation from Kush were an elephant tusk, an okapi, and a vessel with a lid, perhaps containing gold.[60]

The comparison between Ethiopian and Egyptian practices was a matter of interest to Herodotus. Discussing two figures of Sesostris that the Egyptian king had engraved on rocks in Ionia to celebrate a triumph, the historian noted that the equipment and dress were both Egyptian and Ethiopian.[61] He was not certain whether the Egyptians adopted the very ancient custom of circumcision from the Ethiopians or vice versa.[62] In commenting on the Egyptian soldiers who had settled in Ethiopia in the reign of Psamtik I, Herodotus observed that Ethiopians learned Egyptian customs and became milder-mannered by intermixture with Egyptians.[63]

The Athenian dramatists of the fifth century B.C. played to an interest in a distant people brought closer to home by recent experiences: Ethiopian contingents in Xerxes' army and their bows of palm-wood strips, four cubits long, were a reality for some Greeks.[64] Although the Greeks had encountered Ethiopians as enemies in the Persian Wars, there was no specifically anti-black sentiment in Greek drama. In the *Suppliant Maidens* of Aeschylus, the color of the Danaids was not an issue to King Pelasgus and his Argives when they were confronted with a decision on a question that they realized involved the possiblity of war. Most un-Greek in appearance, "black and smitten by the sun," the Danaids, descendants of Io, received asylum in Argos.[65] Exploiting a curiosity about a "far-off country of a black race who lived by the fountains of the sun,"[66] the dramatists turned to legends with African settings. The Memnon story was treated in the *Memnon* and *Psychostasia* of Aeschylus and in the *Aithiopes* of Sophocles.[67] Both Sophocles and Euripides wrote an *Andromeda*;[68] the Busiris legend inspired comedies by Epicharmus, Ephippus, and Mnesimachus and a satyr play by Euripides. The titles and extant fragments of these plays, all of which apparently included Ethiopians, reveal little about the precise treatment of the myths. The vase painters, however, with whom these "Ethiopian" legends were also popular, provided some details as to setting and costumes and, most important in developing the fifth-century concept of an Ethiopian, left no doubt about the physical characteristics of Ethiopians: some were pronouncedly Negroid; others were mulattoes.[69]

In view of the interest in dramatic festivals and the size of the audiences, it is not unlikely that the plays of Aeschylus, Sophocles, and Euripides stimulated a more widespread discussion of Ethiopians in Greece than at any earlier period, except perhaps when reports had first come back from Greek mercenaries and settlers in

Egypt. Following performances of plays on Ethiopian themes, the-
atergoers may well have concerned themselves with related questions such as the significance of "Ethiopian phialai" (fig. 39a-b)
mentioned among offerings to Athena or the reason for the appearance of Ethiopians on the phiale that the statue of Nemesis at
Rhamnus (not far from Marathon) held in its right hand.[70] Were
these Ethiopians related in any way to Homer's blameless Ethiopians? Or what was the identity of the Negro whose image was struck
on the coins of Athens (fig. 40a-b) and Delphi? Was he Delphos, the
son of the Black Woman[71], and did his features resemble those of
the Ethiopians in Xerxes' army? These and similar questions would
not have escaped the attention of curious Greeks.

The Ptolemaic period

After the fifth century very little new was added to the Greek image
of the Ethiopian until the Ptolemaic era. An indication of the kind of
information circulated after the activity of the Ptolemies in Ethiopia
is found in extracts from *On the Erythraean Sea*, a treatise by the
second-century B.C. geographer and historian Agatharchides, whose
sources included accounts of merchants and eye-witnesses as well
as the royal archives in Alexandria. Excerpts from Agatharchides,
surviving in Diodorus and Photius, provided new anthropological
details: one group of Ethiopians was called Simi, because of their
markedly flat noses; the Acridophagi (Locust Eaters) were described
as exceedingly black.[72] Inland Ethiopian tribes, whom Agatharchides located imprecisely in the south, were divided into four
major categories: river tribes who planted sesame and millet, lake
dwellers who garnered reed and soft wood, nomads who lived on
meat and milk, and shore dwellers who fished.[73] Basic Ethiopian
diet was also sometimes reflected in the nomenclature of tribes such
as the Struthophagi (Ostrich Eaters),[74] the Spermatophagi, who ate
nuts and fruits of trees,[75] and the Elephantophagi (Elephant
Eaters).[76] In his account of the Ichthyophagi (Fish Eaters) Agatharchides introduced certain elements of idealization, absent in
Herodotus' earlier record of Ethiopians. Autochthonous people who
wore no clothes and had wives in common, the Ichthyophagi led a
utopian existence, free from want, greed, and envy, which elicited

from Agatharchides moralistic conclusions about their way of life. Unlike Greeks, the Ichthyophagi were not concerned with super- fluities but, rejecting useless things, strove for a divine way of life. With no desire for power, Agatharchides continues, they were not distressed by strife; nor did they imperil their lives by sailing the sea for the sake of gain. Needing little, they suffered little; gaining pos- session of what was sufficient, they sought no more. And they were not governed by laws, for those who are able to live uprightly with- out the sanction of written law need no ordinances.[77]

Agatharchides also mentions other Ethiopians, closer to the everyday reality of the Hellenistic world and a source of concern to the Ptolemies. In preparation for an Ethiopian campaign an un- named Ptolemy, perhaps Epiphanes (205–180 B.C.), had included among his mercenaries five hundred horsemen from Greece. It was no doubt the threat of Ethiopian warriors, skilled in the use of their huge bows and deadly poisonous arrows, that induced an experi- enced regent to offer this advice against undertaking an expedition into Ethiopia: "Why futilely announce an impossible task and pay attention to invisible hopes rather than to manifest dangers?"[78]

The early empire

For a fuller image of the Ethiopian in Ptolemaic times, Diodorus, a historian of the late first century B.C., who used Agatharchides as one of his sources,[79] is a useful supplement for our understanding of the Ptolemaic image of Ethiopians. Some of the "primitive" Ethiopi- ans of Diodorus wore no clothes at all, some covered only their loins, and others their bodies up to the waist. Some were filthy and kept their nails long like beasts, and a few did not believe in any gods at all.[80] In general, says Diodorus, these Ethiopians cultivated none of the practices of civilized life found among the rest of man- kind and their customs were in striking contrast to Greco-Roman practices—differences that Diodorus explains in terms of environ- ment.[81] After describing the effects of the excessive cold of the north on Scythia and its inhabitants, and of the torrid heat on the regions beyond Egypt and the Trogodyte country, Diodorus con- cludes that it was not surprising that "both the fare and the manner of life and the bodies of the inhabitants should differ very much from such as are found among us."[82]

The fourth-century B.C. historian Ephorus had said that some write only about the savage Scythians because they know that the terrible and marvelous are startling, but had insisted that the opposite facts should also be noted.[83] Diodorus noted that some of his sources on both Egypt and Ethiopia had accepted false reports or invented tales to please their readers.[84] Refusing to accept such an approach, in the spirit of Ephorus, Diodorus was not blind to the achievements of other Ethiopians whose reputation for wisdom was great, and whose religious practices made them a kind of chosen people in the eyes of the gods. The peoples who inhabited the island of Meroë and the region adjoining Egypt, according to Diodorus' sources, were considered to be the first of all men and the first to honor the gods whose favor they enjoyed. It was largely because of Ethiopian piety, Diodorus continues, that the gods doomed to failure the attempts of foreign rulers such as Cambyses to invade and occupy their country. These Ethiopians were not only pioneers in religion but also originated many Egyptian customs. From these Ethiopians, in Diodorus' account, the Egyptians, who were colonists sent out by the Ethiopians, derived their beliefs concerning their burial practices and the role of priests, shapes of statues, and forms of writing.[85]

In the early Roman Empire lesser-known regions of both the distant south and the far north were reported to be inhabited by imaginary creatures, perhaps invented by writers such as those whom Diodorus rejected. Included among the inhabitants of inner Africa, according to Pliny the Elder, were the Trogodytae, who had no voices but made squeaking noises; the Blemmyae, who had no heads and their mouths and eyes attached to their chests; the Himantopodes (Strapfoots) with feet resembling leather thongs, who crawled instead of walking; and noseless and mouthless tribes who through a single orifice breathed, ate, and drank by means of oat straws.[86] Pliny acknowledges in another description of inner Africa that he was dealing with unreality by his prefatory statement that he was coming to purely imaginary regions—the land of the Nigroi, whose king was said to have only one eye, the Pamphagi, who ate everything; and the Anthropophagi, who ate human flesh. Similarly, Pliny is apparently expressing his doubt about fabulous creatures of this type when he explains that coastal Ethiopians, the Nisicathae and Nisitae, names meaning three- and four-eyed men, were so designated not because they were physically bizarre but because they were unusually accurate in the use of bow and arrow.[87]

Like other writers in the early empire, however, Pliny also followed Ephorus' caveat on inaccurate reporting and continued the old tradition of writing about the more familiar Ethiopians, whose wisdom and "priority" of institutions came to be important elements in the image of Ethiopians current in the empire. Ethiopian wisdom, according to Pliny, was to be attributed to the mobility of the southern climate in the same manner as the fierceness of northerners was to their harsh environment.[88] Lucian informs us that Ethiopians first gave the doctrine of astrology to men and, "being in all else wiser than other men," transmitted their discoveries about the heavens to the Egyptians.[89] In the *Aethiopica* of Heliodorus, a high priest of Isis states that during a visit to the Ethiopian court he had enriched his Egyptian knowledge with Ethiopian wisdom.[90]

Echoes of the glory of the Twenty-fifth Dynasty were still heard in the early empire and were reported with apparent admiration. Strabo included Tearco (Taharqa) the Ethiopian among the world's great conquerors, with Sesostris, Psamtik, and the Persians from Cyrus to Xerxes, and cites Megasthenes as his source for the statement that Taharqa advanced as far as Europe.[91] The Sabacos of Diodorus resembles very closely that of Herodotus with one exception: Diodorus adds that in piety and uprightness Sabacos far surpassed his predecessors, and contrasts Ethiopian justice with the harshness, injustice, and arrogance of the Egyptian Amasis.[92] Freedom-loving Ethiopians, according to Seneca, who had talked with centurions after their return from the Ethiopian mission under Nero's auspices, rejected Cambyses' threat of slavery and, instead of accepting servitude with outstretched arms, sent envoys and replied in words befitting the free and insulting to kings.[93]

The importance, if only propagandistic, that Augustus attached to Petronius' Ethiopian campaigns is perhaps suggested by the inclusion of his Ethiopian victories in the official record of his administration and achievements known as the *Res Gestae Divi Augusti* (Deeds of the Deified Augustus). Copies of this document, originally engraved on bronze tablets outside the emperor's mausoleum in Rome, and set up in some if not all the provinces, were constant reminders to the Roman world of the Meroïtic threat to Egypt's southern boundary.[94] The many terracotta figurines of Negro warriors from the Roman period found in Egypt (fig. 41) provide vivid illustrations of Rome's Ethiopian adversaries mentioned by authors of the early Roman Empire.[95] In spite of Augustus' difficulties with African blacks, Vergil did not hesitate to pay tribute to the assistance that Ethiopians had given to Rome's ancestors in the Trojan War. Aeneas, as he gazed with deep emotion at scenes depicted on the outer walls of Dido's temple at Carthage, recognized himself and the armor of his black ally, Memnon.[96] In his account of Augustus' Ethiopian campaign, Pliny pointed out that Ethiopia had not been made a desert by the armies of Rome, but that the region, a powerful and famous country down to the Trojan War, once ruler of Syria and the Mediterranean coasts, had been exhausted by a series of wars with Egypt.[97]

Another important source for the image of Ethiopians projected during the early empire was Josephus, whose *Jewish Antiquities* included several episodes highlighting Ethiopia's prominence as an independent state of considerable military power. Enlarging upon the reference to Moses' Kushite wife in the Old Testament, Josephus added a story of the love of an Ethiopian princess for her father's enemy in time of war. The Ethiopians, according to Josephus, invaded Egypt, repulsed an Egyptian counterattack, and marched as far north as Memphis and the sea, conquering as they went. Only after the Egyptians, in response to word from God, appointed Moses as their general were the Ethiopians driven back to their capital and forced to abandon hope of subduing Egypt. As Moses was besieging the Ethiopian capital, Josephus continues, Tharbis, daughter of the Ethiopian king, fell madly in love with Moses and sent him a proposal of marriage, which he accepted upon condition that she surrender the city. Moses fulfilled his promise to marry the princess once the city was captured, celebrated the nuptials, and led the victorious army back to Egypt.[98]

With slight variations, Josephus describes several other martial events involving Ethiopians mentioned in the Old Testament. Among these are two Ethiopian campaigns in Palestine: the sack of Jerusalem by Isokos (Shishak), with many tens of thousands of troops and 400,000 infantrymen, most of whom were Libyans and Ethiopians;[99] and the invasion by Zaraios (Zerah), king of the Ethiopians, at the head of an army of 900,000 foot soldiers, 100,000 horsemen, and 300 chariots, and his defeat by Asa.[100] Sennacherib, the Assyrian king, failed in Egypt, according to Josephus, because as he was about to attack Pelusium he received word that Tharsikes (Taharqa), king of the Ethiopians, was coming to aid the Egyptians, and he decided to withdraw.[101]

Other "scriptural Ethiopians" appear in *Jewish Antiquities*. The Queen of Sheba becomes the Queen of Egypt and Ethiopia, "thoroughly trained in wisdom and admirable in other things,"[102] and an Ethiopian servant of Zedekiah is responsible for saving Jeremiah by convincing the king whose favor he enjoyed that the prophet had been wronged.[103] Josephus retold Ethiopian history at a time when blacks were well-known anthropological types and brought to the attention of the early empire some themes that Christian exegetes were to use frequently in interpreting the mystery of the Church—the marriage of Moses to the Ethiopian woman; Ebed-melech, the rescuer of the prophet Jeremiah; and the visit of the Queen of Sheba to Solomon.[104] At the same time, *Jewish Antiquities* reinforced the recurrent image of black warriors and their widely respected kingdom, and may have reminded the historian's contemporaries of events closer to their own era: the Ethiopian attack on the Romans in Egypt at the time of Augustus had been foreshadowed by the ancient Ethiopian invasion of Egypt; and the wise Queen of Sheba had a later counterpart in the Ethiopian queen, whose ambassadors were diplomatically so skillful as to gain from Augustus all their requests.[105]

Late impressions of Ethiopians

One of the last works in classical literature to treat at some length an Ethiopian theme is the *Aethiopica* of Heliodorus. Hydaspes, the king of the Ethiopians in the third- or fourth-century romance, is a model of wisdom and justice; he prefers not to put men to death; in the tradition of Piye, he instructs his warriors to refrain from slaughter and to take the enemy alive.[106] When his foe pleads for survival, Hydaspes grants mercy. In the same charitable spirit he proclaims, as he glances at the bleeding Oroondates, the viceroy of the king of Persia: "A noble thing it is to surpass an enemy in battle when he is standing, but in generosity when he has fallen"[107]—a sentiment Vergilian in spirit and reminiscent of Anchises' words, "Spare the humble and subdue the proud."[108] In gratitude for the Ethiopian's decision to allow him to return to his province, Oroondates renders obeisance to Hydaspes, an honor that Persians reserved for their king, and calls the Ethiopian ruler the most just of mortals for having granted him life and freedom instead of death or slavery.[109] Like the Macrobian king who did not covet the land of others, Hydaspes is content with the natural boundaries of the Cataracts and, having accomplished his mission, returns to Ethiopia.[110] Though on the point of following a tradition of sacrificing foreign prisoners to the gods, Hydaspes, convinced by the chief of his advisers (called Gymnosophists) of the inappropriateness of such a practice, persuades his people to renounce human sacrifice.[111]

In the fourth century, the epic poet Quintus of Smyrna revived the glorious exploits of Memnon and his black soldiers.[112] The arrival of a countless host of Ethiopians brings joy to the beleaguered Trojans, who flock to the streets to see them;[113] hope is rekindled that the Ethiopians might burn the Greek ships.[114] The Ethiopians of Quintus are foremost in battle, killing many a warrior.[115] Nor are they forgotten by heaven after Memnon's death because a god speeds them off from the battlefield, and as they mourn the death of their king, Dawn changes them into birds, afterwards called "the Memnons," who continue to utter wailing cries as they fly about Memnon's tomb.[116]

The classical image of blacks in retrospect

Certain lines of the Greek and Roman profile of Ethiopians remained basically unchanged from Homer to the end of classical literature—and the image was essentially favorable. Following Ptolemaic exploration of Nubia, reports reached the Greeks about hitherto lesser-known Ethiopians, far to the south of Egypt. The extant excerpts of Agatharchides, the first to describe these southern tribes in detail, show that there was no tendency, even upon first discovery, to barbarize these Ethiopians. On the contrary, Agatharchides idealized some of them in a kind of philosophical treatise on "primitives." Diodorus, whose picture of Ethiopians was one of the most comprehensive in classical literature, adopted a balanced method of reporting, without generalizing about nudity or community of wives and without giving undue emphasis to the exceptional. While not omitting practices of "primitive" Ethiopians that were strikingly unusual from the Greco-Roman point of view, Diodorus also included an account of those Ethiopians whom his sources regarded as the *first of all men* and as the originators of divine rituals most pleasing to the gods. Even after the Greeks and Romans had encountered Ethiopians as enemies, classical writers continued to treat without rancor ancient "Ethiopian" themes—military power, love of freedom and justice, piety, and wisdom.

Throughout the history of classical literature, elements of idealization and unreality appear in some descriptions of distant peoples, especially those in the far north and south. The distant regions of Scythia and Ethiopia, for example, were at times the homes of fabulous creatures or wild and ferocious tribes; at other times the inhabitants were characterized as paragons of justice.[117] But the view that most of the Ethiopians of classical literature were unrelated to reality needs reconsideration. Even Homer's blameless Ethiopians may have stemmed from reports of Ethiopian piety, and the poet's black, woolly-haired Eurybates[118] may have reflected an awareness of a black power on the southern edge of the Greek universe. Nubia, as far south as Meroë, was a region often as well known in the Greco-Roman world as it had been to the Egyptians. In fact, Africanists have found many observations of classical writers of considerable value in the reconstruction of the Napatan-Meroïtic Kingdom of Kush.

From the time of Herodotus onward, classical authors, despite some unreliable reporting and occasional fanciful creations, were often dealing with African realities and were much more knowledgeable than has been realized. Herodotus was the first of several writers to reflect an awareness of the Ethiopian Dynasty. The historian's account of Sabacos' piety is reminiscent of the Napatan's victorious Piye and is corroborated to some extent by Shabaka's interest in restoring religious texts of the Old Kingdom, attested by inscriptional evidence.[119] Herodotus' mention of Ethiopians in the population of Cyprus may have been based on knowledge of an Ethiopian presence dating back at least to Amasis' conquest of the island in the Twenty-sixth Dynasty.[120] In his description of Cambyses' plans for an Ethiopian campaign, Herodotus describes a "table of the sun,"[121] said to have been a meadow outside the city where boiled meat was placed by magistrates for whoever wanted to partake of it. The historian in this passage, according to specialists on Meroë, has provided an apt description of the site of the Sun Temple, located outside the city of Meroë in an area that can be described appropriately as a meadow because vegetation still grows there more readily than in the surrounding plain.[122] Herodotus' account of Macrobian expertise in archery and his description of the bows of Xerxes' Ethiopian auxiliaries[123]—like Heliodorus' later description of the Ethiopians' unerring skill in hitting their target, their adversaries' eyes—[124] point to an ancient military tradition in the south: the bow had been the typical weapon of the Nubians since the days of the black archers at Gebelein and Assiut,[125] and as late as the seventh century A.D. Nubian bowmen, known to the Arab invaders as "pupil smiters," were respected for their skill in blinding their opponents.[126]

Lucian's statement that Ethiopians invented astrology[127] may have stemmed in part from the reports of travelers who had visited Meroë. Astronomical equipment and graffiti representing actual sketches of astronomical calculations, dating from the second century B.C., have been found at Meroë.[128] Remains of Meroïtic temples show that astronomical orientation was an important factor in the layout of these structures.[129] It is tempting to suggest that Greek and Roman visitors to Meroë, impressed by their "discoveries" at the southern periphery of the world, circulated the belief that astrology was an Ethiopian gift to mankind and gave rise to further speculation that a number of Egyptian institutions had an Ethiopian origin.

Much of what has sometimes been classified as an "idealization" of Ethiopians, when not actually a reflection of facts, may have been based on reports of what Herodotus heard at Elephantine or of informants such as the Ethiopian ambassadors with whom Dio-

dorus spoke.[130] Ethiopian partisans would certainly have emphasized the justice of the southerners' cause and their efforts to protect
their country from foreign exploitation. Sympathetic references to
Ethiopian justice and resistance to foreign aggression such as those
of Herodotus, Diodorus, and Seneca, therefore, should perhaps be
regarded as a tribute to the objectivity of classical writers in
recording the Ethiopian point of view rather than as the idealization
of an unknown, distant people. Finally, the Greco-Roman image of
blacks, even if at times idealized or not always based on historical
fact, must have had an enormous impact on the day-to-day attitudes
toward blacks. What is significant is not the objective truth of ancient reports, but the frame of mind that made them possible. Perceptions are often influential in shaping social attitudes and are important factors to be considered in assessing the Mediterranean
view of blacks.

Nubia was perceived by its contemporaries as an independent
country, rich in coveted resources, inhabited to a large extent by
dark-skinned and Negroid peoples, who from time to time played a
significant role in the international politics of the day. Nubia as a
military power on the periphery of the Mediterranean world was by
far the most prominent feature of the ancient profile of blacks. The
ability of Nubia, a nation of skilled archers, to defend itself from
foreign exploitation gained the respect of its enemies, even of Egyptians and Assyrians in spite of the often exaggerated and contemptuous claims of their "official" accounts. The services of Ethiopian
warriors undoubtedly won the gratitude of others for whose causes
they fought in various parts of the Mediterranean world. The
Twenty-fifth Dynasty was not only known among contemporaries,
but its accomplishments were considered worthy of note and admiration by later chroniclers. The requests of Baal of Tyre and Hezekiah of Judah for Napatan assistance illustrate Asiatic awareness
of the dynasty's influence. The Book of Nahum recalled the glory of
the Napatan kingdom long after its fall at the hands of Assyrians.
That Taharqa was still regarded as a great military leader six hundred years after his death is evident from Strabo's list of famed
world conquerors.

It is important to emphasize that the overall, but especially the
more detailed Greco-Roman, view of blacks was highly positive.

Initial, favorable impressions were not altered, in spite of later accounts of wild tribes in the far south and even after encounters with blacks had become more frequent. There was clear-cut respect among Mediterranean peoples for Ethiopians and their way of life. And, above all, the ancients did not stereotype all blacks as primitives defective in religion and culture.

4

TOWARD AN UNDER- STANDING OF THE ANCIENT VIEW

4

Color prejudice has been a major issue in the modern world. W. E. B. Du Bois called it the "problem of the twentieth century,"[1] and D. B. Saddington, among others, notes that racial difficulties are at their worst when associated with differences in skin color.[2] Notable, therefore, is the fact that the ancient world did not make color the focus of irrational sentiments or the basis for uncritical evaluation. The ancients did accept the institution of slavery as a fact of life; they made ethnocentric judgments of other societies; they had narcissistic canons of physical beauty; the Egyptians distinguished between themselves, "the people," and outsiders; and the Greeks called foreign cultures barbarian. Yet nothing comparable to the virulent color prejudice of modern times existed in the ancient world.[3] This is the view of most scholars who have examined the evidence and who have come to conclusions such as these: the ancients did not fall into the error of biological racism;[4] black skin color was not a sign of inferiority;[5] Greeks and Romans did not establish color as an obstacle to integration in society;[6] and ancient society was one that "for all its faults and failures never made color the basis for judging a man."[7]

To some commentators, however, a few ancient texts suggest color prejudice, or at least the germ of anti-black bias. Some, for example, regard as pejorative statements in classical authors that point to a preference for northern or "white" rather than for southern or "dark" beauties. Such interpretations, however, do not mention that the ancients themselves recognized that the criteria for beauty varied from nation to nation, and that those in the predominantly white societies of Greece and Rome having preference for "black" beauty did not hesitate to say so. Parenthetically, it is questionable whether individuals should be called "racist" because they accept aesthetic canons prevailing in their country.

There has also been at times a tendency to read modern racial concepts into ancient documents and to see color prejudice where none existed. Scholars have made these observations: the ugliness of the Negro seems to have appealed alike to sculptor, engraver, and painter;[8] "plastic" vases are always best when the subject, like the Negro's head, is itself grotesque;[9] or Negroes in classical art are often near caricatures or outright examples of the comic.[10] But those scholars who have allowed ancient art to speak for itself argue that the so-called ugliness or comic exists primarily in the minds of the modern beholders, not in the eyes of the ancient artists, and that Negro subjects are among some of the finest and most sympathetically executed pieces to have come from the workshops of ancient artists.[11] The view of blacks as the equivalent of slaves or savages has sometimes given rise to an unwillingness to accept the implications of the ancient evidence. In spite of the widespread repute of blacks as mercenaries in antiquity, for example, Xerxes' black contingent in the Persian Wars has been described as a "humble and almost grotesque auxiliary."[12] A remarkable incredulity appears in the following observation on the rule of the Twenty-fifth Ethiopian Dynasty in Egypt: "In the place of a native Egyptian pharaoh or of the usurping Libyans the throne of Egypt was occupied by a Negro king from Ethiopia! But his dominion was not for long."[13]

In general, the pattern of black-white relations in the ancient world differed markedly from that of later societies which have attached great importance to skin color. The probable reasons for the attitudes toward blacks in antiquity have never been adequately explored. Such an inquiry is in itself worth undertaking, but an examination of the ancient black-white racial pattern in the light of modern research on the origin and nature of prejudice is also instructive. Though social, economic, and demographic factors have obviously differed in many respects, some comparisons of racial attitudes in the ancient and modern world are not without value. The perception of blacks, for example, in modern northwest Africa (the Maghreb), a region where blacks and whites have encountered each other for centuries, has been similar in some respects to that of the ancient world, while the view of blacks in countries that have lacked the experience of Mediterranean societies has often been negative. Thus a consideration of the experience of blacks in dissimilar milieus may provide a key to understanding attitudes toward color in antiquity and may throw some light on why color, in itself neutral and meaningless, has come to assume such great importance in the self-image of many peoples.

The Size of the Black Population

The proportion of blacks in predominantly white societies is often included among factors that have contributed to the development of color prejudice. An appropriate starting point for this analysis, therefore, is a consideration of the size of the black element in the population of ancient Mediterranean societies.

The exact ratio of blacks to whites in various parts of the ancient world is not known and, because of the lack of overall statistics, cannot be precisely determined. We would be better informed as to the number of blacks and their descendants if the ancients had considered color of sufficient significance to mention it more frequently in referring to blacks and their families. In general, ethnic tags were applied in antiquity to persons of pronounced Negroid characteristics much less often than in many postclassical societies, and only occasionally to mulattoes and others of mixed black-white extraction. In spite of the shortcomings of the evidence, a number of factors suggest that blacks were much more numerous than has been recognized. Frequent notices in ancient documents attest that for centuries blacks were well-known types in Mediterranean regions. The few instances that provide figures in the hundreds or thousands are valuable for general estimates of blacks in similar cases in which numbers are not given.[14] It would be hazardous to generalize on the basis of such small samples, but in view of the scope of the military operations in which blacks participated—the centuries-old employment of mercenaries in Egyptian armies, the encounters of Meroïtes with the Ptolemies and Romans, the presence of Ethiopians in the Persian and Carthaginian forces and in other military conflicts in northeast and northwest Africa—the few available figures take on greater significance.

Iconographical evidence has not been given enough weight in the assessment of the black population. The tendency has been to give attention only to the so-called pure Negro and to ignore almost entirely blacks of less pronounced Negroid characteristics, with the result that the picture of blacks in antiquity has been as unrealistic and distorted as a study of the black population in the United States or Brazil would be if restricted to a consideration of "pure" Negroes. The works of artists that have come down to us are only a small fraction of what must have existed: all the more significant, then, are the large number and wide variety of Negroid types that have survived from every major period of ancient art. If it is also kept in mind how often it is possible to relate the blacks of ancient artists to specific facts or historical events, it is apparent that the value of iconography has been greatly underestimated. Though obviously much larger in Egypt than elsewhere, the black population in other Mediterranean areas, especially in northwest Africa and Italy, was probably also greater than traditional estimates.

Several scholars have maintained that the small size of the black population in the ancient world was a factor in minimizing racial hostility. Illustrative of these views are the following: blacks were few in number except in Egypt and, hence, there was no political or economic competition between whites and blacks; hostility would have arisen if there had been more blacks, even though free; the population of blacks in Rome did not correspond to the threshold of intolerance that some modern sociologists attempt to define.[15] These opinions are in themselves debatable; and more so if my interpretation of the evidence as to size of the black population is correct. Further, with respect to the question of numbers, the importance of Egypt is often overlooked: people from three continents often formed their views of blacks on the basis of what they saw and heard in Egypt, where for centuries the black element in the population was obviously sizable. Observations of Greeks and Romans who resided in or visited Egypt show no indication of hostility toward blacks: in fact, writers like Diodorus, the historian of the second half of the first century B.C., and Origen, the Christian author of the third century A.D.,[16] did much to further a highly favorable image of blacks.

In antiquity the black population was at least large enough to satisfy what P. L. van den Berghe considers the most important necessary condition for the development of racism: "the presence in sufficient numbers of two or more groups that look different enough so that at least some of their members can be easily classifiable."[17]

Still, intense color prejudice did not arise. The evidence from the ancient world seems to confirm the views of scholars who hold that the "numbers theory" of the origin of color prejudice must be used with care.[18] Philip Mason cautions against "attempting to fix any exact proportion at which certain results will follow." The state of Bahia, though located in a section of northeastern Brazil where Negroes have been most numerous, is the region in which prejudice against colored peoples has been, in the opinion of many Brazilian specialists, the slightest, while in regions like São Paulo, where Negroes are proportionately fewer, color prejudice has been more pronounced.[19] The ancient pattern as a whole would seem to have resembled that of modern northwest Africa, where, in spite of a sizable black element in the population, color has not played as significant a role in the white man's vision of blacks as in some other areas of the modern world.[20] The argument that color prejudice is an inevitable consequence of numbers finds little support in the experience of the ancient world.

First Impressions of Blacks

An inclination to discriminate on the basis of readily observable physical differences, it has been suggested, is lessened in white societies that have always had blacks in their midst.[21] The hypothesis that a feeling of common humanity is generated by white-black familiarity over the years merits consideration because in the ancient world, as in later northwest Africa, several predominantly white peoples had prolonged contacts with blacks.

We have seen that populations of dark pigmentations were nothing novel to ancient Mediterranean peoples. Negroes were present in Egypt as early as the middle of the third millennium B.C.; black mercenaries lived in upper Egypt not far from Thebes (Luxor) at the beginning of the second millennium B.C. and, farther north, shortly thereafter. And outside Africa the Negroid type was known in Crete early in the second millennium B.C. In the ninth century B.C., Zerah and his Kushites and later Taharqa led black troops into Asia. Blacks were among the first foreign peoples whom many Greek colonists and mercenaries encountered in the sixth century B.C.; and they were known to the Romans as early as the Carthaginian Wars.

The inhabitants of Egypt during the Pharaonic, Ptolemaic, and Roman periods not only developed an acquaintance with blacks in Egypt itself but also, through regular contacts of various sorts with the south, acquired a knowledge of Nubia and its populations. White-black contacts, however, were not limited to northeast Africa. The ancients, and especially the Romans, were also well acquainted with dark-skinned peoples living in northwest Africa.

In short, in the Mediterranean world the black man was seldom a strange, unknown being. In this respect the ancient situation differed strikingly, for example, from that in countries such as England, where the powerful impact the Africans' color made upon sixteenth-century Englishmen resulted from the abrupt nature of their contacts with blacks: one of the fairest nations on earth was suddenly brought face to face with one of the blackest of mankind.[22] In England color became the basis for discrimination. In the Maghreb, on the other hand, with its long history of black-white contacts, bitter hostility toward blacks did not arise. The pattern of the ancient white-black encounters, therefore, may have been a factor in the formation of attitudes toward blacks in antiquity.

First impressions often have a significant role in the formation of images, sometimes an effect of considerable duration. Among the earliest blacks depicted by artists of the Old Kingdom were prisoners of war, some of the first in a long line of black warriors to resist Egyptian aggression in Kush or to serve in pharaonic armies at various periods from 2000 B.C. on. The experience of Egyptians with black soldiers was not unique. Warriors were among the first blacks encountered not only by Egyptians but also by Asiatics and Europeans. A majority of the first blacks whom many whites came to know both inside and outside Africa were not "savages" or slaves but, like the whites themselves, soldiers protecting their own territory against foreign invasion or pursuing their national or personal interests in other lands. Nothing in these initial contacts points to a pejorative view of blacks. On the contrary, black soldiers commanded the respect of peoples beyond Nubia at various times from the second millennium B.C. until the early Roman Empire. Among many Mediterraneans the first and continuing image of blacks was that of a respected ally or an enemy, often a formidable foe.

Another first impression of tremendous importance in its impact on attitudes toward blacks in the Greek and Roman world was the Homeric image of Ethiopians. The influence of Homer's blameless Ethiopians, the most distant of men, favorites of the gods, is the subject of B. M. Warmington's penetrating observation on the first Ethiopians in European literature: "It cannot be said what dim memory of the Bronze Age lies behind Homer's few but much discussed lines about the 'blameless Ethiopians' ... Their real importance, given the place of the Homeric epics in the Greek consciousness, lies in the fact that they were there at all; it was inevitable that in later Greek times, geographers and philosophers would discover what would explain and amplify the Homeric references, and in particular the religious practices which would account for the favor of the gods. The fact that these as recorded are in no way remarkable, and that some Ethiopians lived in a state of savagery, made no difference to the generally favorable judgement."[23] Whatever the origin and full significance of Homer's blameless Ethiopians, and whatever their precise physical characteristics, Ethiopian-Olympian consortia and pious, just Ethiopians were not forgotten, with vestiges of these Ethiopians appearing in late classical and early Christian authors as well. The initially favorable view of Ethiopians was reinforced long after African Negroes had become an everyday reality, in environmental explanations of racial differences, in ideas of the unity of mankind, and in the exegeses of Christian writers. And there was nothing in the daily experiences of blacks as slaves, freedmen, or freemen that did not confirm formal and informal expressions of these views.

In striking contrast was the attitude toward blacks and their color in some later societies where first impressions derived from different circumstances. An account of the first English voyages to Africa in the mid-sixteenth century, for example, described Negroes as a people of "beastly living, without a God, laws, religion, or common wealth; and so scorched and vexed with the heate of the sunne, that in many places they curse it when it riseth"[24]—obviously vastly different from the descriptions of Ethiopians in Homer, Herodotus, or Agatharchides. The Negro's color became in the English mind, W. D. Jordan has observed, the identification of a native of a distant continent of African peoples radically defective in religion, libidinous, bestial, a source of slaves.[25] An early, partly fictional and partly factual response to Africa characterized much of the Englishman's understanding of Africa for two hundred and fifty years. In England the myths of Africa, James Walvin emphasizes, were "to prove more resilient and influential than its truths."[26]

In antiquity slavery was independent of race or class, and by far the vast majority of the thousands of slaves was white, not black. The identification of blackness with slavery did not develop. No single ethnic group was associated with slave status or with the descendants of slaves. The Negro as slave or freedman was in a no more disadvantageous position than anyone else unfortunate enough to be captured as a prisoner of war or to be enslaved for some other reason. It has often been noted that anti-black racism developed or increased in intensity after black and slave had become synonymous. In the New World, after the emergence of the doctrine that "a slave cannot be a white man" and of color as the token of slave status,[27] "the most powerful and persistent claims were put forward," as M. I. Finley has pointed out, "for the 'naturalness' of slavery, with ample quotation from the Bible, and moral arguments for the *abolition* of slavery were fully mustered for the first time."[28]

In fact, it no doubt was an important stage in the beginning of the end of slavery when slavery became identified with the Negro only. "When the definition of slavery was symbolized by the Negro," W. L. Westermann remarked, "it spelled the death knell of slavery itself within the European cultural area."[29] A new issue arose: Why the Negro only? Answers to this question gave rise to all kinds of theories as to the innate inferiority of Negroes and to racial stereotypes nonexistent in ancient society. In attempts to justify slavery, later Christians maintained, Roger Bastide notes, that God punished Negroes with a black skin and, against a background of black-white symbolism, "invented causes for the malady, intended to justify in their own eyes a process of production based upon the exploitation of Negro labor."[30] Such a use of a black-white symbolism was completely alien, as we shall see, to the spirit of the formidable exegesis in which early Christians made the Ethiopians representative of the totality of Gentiles.

To summarize this point, the ancient world never developed a concept of the equivalence of slave and black; nor did it create theories to prove that blacks were more suited than others to slavery. The importance of this difference was underscored early in the century by the Earl of Cromer, who raised the question of whether "a differentiation between the habits of thought of moderns and ancients may, in some degree, be established on the ground that the former have only enslaved the colored races, whereas the latter doomed all conquered people indiscriminately to slavery." The close identification of slavery with difference of color encouraged the idea of white supremacy and fostered racial antipathy.[31]

Images of Nubia in Contemporary Societies

In the modern world the image of Africans in the minds of whites has often been considered a major factor in the development of color prejudice. Edward Shils, for example, has observed that one of the simplest and most obvious reasons for the great importance color has assumed in the self-imagery of many peoples is that it is an easy means of distinguishing "between those from the periphery and those from the center of particular societies and of the world society." "Differences of pigmentation," Shils continues, "symbolize or indicate contemporaneous differences between present wealth and power and present poverty and weakness, between present fame and present obscurity, between present eminence in intellectual creativity and present intellectual unproductiveness."[32] This observation on color as the focus of complex sentiments provides another useful basis for looking at the image of blacks in antiquity. What was the image of Nubia in contemporary Mediterranean societies? What were common opinions of Nubia's material resources, military and political position, its cultural and intellectual attainments?

Nubia's natural resources were items in great demand among the inhabitants of the Nile Valley, who sought access to products within Nubia itself or available to Nubia indirectly through the control of traffic in goods from east or central Africa. Wishing to profit as middlemen in the flow of trade, Nubians responded to the commercial or imperial ambitions of their northern neighbors by a variety of countermeasures. During periods of Egypt's internal military or political difficulties, Nubia often took advantage of Egyptian disunity to promote its own commercial and military interests, meeting with substantial success as early as the Second Intermediate Period. About the age of the composition of the Homeric poems and the time of the traditional founding of Rome, the Napatans were already emerging as a successful and triumphant people: in Robin Hallett's words, "for the first and indeed the only time in history, a state based on the interior of Africa played an active part in the politics of the Mediterranean."[33] Thus it is not surprising that Isaiah describes the Kushites as a great and formidable nation, or that historians like Herodotus and Diodorus looked back to Sabacos as a model king, or that in retrospect Taharqa appeared to Megasthenes and Strabo as a great conqueror.[34] The Ethiopian military presence continued to be felt in the Ptolemaic world. At various times during the occupation of Egypt until late in the sixth century A.D., the Romans found southern opposition a threat to their boundaries, as the Egyptians and Ptolemies had earlier.

In short, the Napatan-Meroïtic Kingdom of Kush, though experiencing foreign occupation from time to time in its thousand-year history, was able to maintain its territorial integrity with remarkable success against powerful nations. The contemporaries of Nubia, far from regarding that country as materially poor or politically and militarily weak, were clearly aware of its resources and its role in the politics of the day. In addition, some Greek and Roman authors wrote sympathetically of Ethiopia's freedom-loving independence and hatred of foreign aggression.[35]

Another factor responsible for the importance of color in the self-imagery of peoples has been the view of blacks as culturally backward. It is instructive, therefore, to refer briefly to cultural highlights of the Napatan and Meroïtic Kingdoms of Kush. The rulers of the Twenty-fifth Dynasty regarded themselves as perpetuators of the pharaonic traditions. They patronized Egyptian gods and shrines, renovated existing temples, built new structures, and restored ancient texts. To many Egyptians, Napatans appeared "Egyptian," not foreign. The later Meroïtes, though heavily indebted to the Egyptians throughout their history in language, religion, and art, gradually developed their own distinctive writing, worshiped their own gods, and created their own style in architecture, sculpture, and pottery.[36] As early as the fifth century B.C.

Herodotus described Meroë as a great city, the capital of the other Ethiopians.[37] Meroë at the time of the ruler Ergamenes in the third century B.C. was a Nubian Alexandria, which saw a renaissance of temple building paralleling the outburst of construction in Ptolemaic and Roman Egypt.[38] As late as the first century B.C. Ethiopians were presented to the Greco-Roman world by Diodorus as among civilization's "pioneers," and by writers of the early Roman Empire as renowned for their wisdom and for their fame in astrology.[39]

It is clear that Nubia, though located on the geographic periphery of the ancient world, was neither considered culturally backward nor sufficiently different from central Mediterranean societies to warrant the extreme contrasts between blacks and whites that Shils links to the development of color prejudice in the modern world. In the eighteenth and nineteenth centuries, as a result of the cultural differences perceived by whites of European stock between themselves and black colonials whom they ruled, many whites associated poverty, inefficiency, and backwardness with non-whites and attached strong emotions to physical differences.[40] Among the ancients, similar associations of color with material poverty, military weakness, political insignificance, and cultural unproductivity did not exist.

Awareness of Color

No single ancient document treats in detail the attitudes of whites toward the color of the black man's skin. Greek and Roman sources, however, are instructive on this subject, particularly when they are examined in the light of modern research on color awareness, standards of beauty, and color symbolism.

The Egyptians, whose contacts with Nubia dated back to the Old Kingdom, did not usually designate Kushites by color terms. Though the monarchs of the Twenty-fifth Dynasty had their skin painted dark-brown in reliefs and their Nubian features clearly delineated by the sculptors,[41] they mentioned neither their own color nor that of the lighter-skinned Egyptians. Piye, for example, in his triumphal stele made no reference to color: he apparently did not regard himself as a champion of black peoples who had overturned their former white masters. Egyptians and Nubians had for centuries been accustomed to the gradations in skin color among the inhabitants of the Nile Valley and hence saw nothing unusual in the differences.

The first to call special attention to the Nubian's blackness were peoples living outside Africa: the color of the Kushites gave rise to a proverb in the Old Testament, and the Greeks invented a color term to describe the Nubians. Though obviously aware of the Nubians' color, however, neither the writers of the Old Testament nor classical authors attached any basic significance to it. Ethiopians do not astonish Greeks because of their blackness and their different physical appearance: such a fear, Agatharchides wrote, ceases at childhood.[42] This statement was not only an accurate assessment of Greek reaction to the Ethiopians' color, but also a sound observation on an aspect of child behavior that has been studied by modern psychologists. "Four-year-olds," according to Gordon Allport, "are normally interested, curious, and appreciative of differences in racial groups."[43] Alan Marsh, in a study on the awareness of racial differences in British and West African children living in Britain, found that the critical age of racial curiosity seems to be around three to three and a half years for the children he studied.[44] In other words, it is perfectly normal for a white child living in a predominantly white society to notice the color of blacks. The reaction of an African child, upon first contacts with whites, is similar and equally innocent. Reporting on his experience in African villages previously unvisited by Europeans, the explorer David Livingstone wrote that the moment a child met them he would "take to his heels in agony of terror" and that the mother, alarmed by the child's wild outcries, would rush out of the hut and dart back again "at the first glimpse of the same fearful apparition."[45]

An initial reaction, even of fear, is normally short-lived in children, according to social psychologists, and may not necessarily have a bearing upon the patterns of later attitudes. There is a strong indication, Marsh concludes, that "whilst the development of 'race values' in children is logically contingent upon knowledge of racial differences, the obverse is not necessarily true. That is to say, children can *know* all about racial differences but do not *necessarily* attach value judgments to them, especially those leading to the formation of racial stereotypes, *unless* they are exposed to socializing forces characterized by overt racial consciousness and/or hostility."[46] In the setting of his study, Marsh noted that "such socializing forces were absent . . . overt race values, beyond those affective bonds formed in personal relationships, were also absent in children."[47] Likewise, Greek and Roman children lived in an atmosphere in which the Negroid type was well known but in which marked hostility to blacks was not a characteristic of the society; there was no reason for a child or even a parent to attach special significance to differences in color or to think that blacks were *fundamentally* different.

In Marsh's investigation a British foster parent of an African child, when his own child remarked for the first time that his African foster brother was still dirty after a bath, explained that his visitor had come from a hot country where the strong sunshine made everyone black.[48] It is possible that a Greek or Roman parent, in response to a child's curiosity about an Ethiopian's color, gave either a mythological or a "scientific" explanation, perhaps both: the story of Phaethon who lost control of his father's chariot and, by coming close to earth, blackened the skin and curled the hair of the Ethiopians; or some version of the environment theory setting forth the effects of climate on northern and southern peoples.[49] Such explanations would have satisfied the curiosity of a Greek or Roman child as effectively as the British answer in Marsh's study: no serious value judgment would have been attached to the Ethiopian's blackness.

In summary, by his observation that fear of Ethiopians ceased at childhood, Agatharchides was merely recording an aspect of child behavior noted by many psychologists since his time—the normal reaction of young children to differences in skin color. He was not setting forth, as Albrecht Dihle has suggested, a theory of aversion to the black man's color rooted in childhood.[50]

The somatic norm image

The Greeks and Romans, like other peoples before and after them, had narcissistic canons of physical beauty. In referring to ethnocentric standards for judging beauty, H. Hoetink uses the term "somatic norm image," which he defines as "the complex of physical (somatic) characteristics which are accepted by a group as its norm and ideal," pointing out that each group considers itself aesthetically superior to others.[51] As an illustration of the somatic norm image, Hoetink mentions a central African creation myth in which the Negro regards himself as perfectly cooked but the white man as underdone because of a defect in the Creator's oven where people were fashioned from clay.[52] Similarly, the Greeks and Romans noted that criteria of beauty varied from people to people. Philostratus remarked that Indians esteemed white less than black because, he implied, black was the color of Indians.[53] Dio Chrysostom's discourse on beauty raised the question as to whether there was not a foreign type of beauty just as there was a Hellenic type.[54] Sextus Empiricus noted that men differed in definitions of beauty—Ethiopians preferring the blackest and most flat-nosed; Persians, the whitest and the most hooked-nose; and others considering those intermediate in color and features as the most beautiful.[55]

What were the Greek and Roman "canons" and their significance for attitudes toward the Ethiopians? The combined Platonic, Lucretian, and Ovidian statements of the classical norm image indicate, in general, a preference for a middle point between the extremes.[56] Lovers in classical poetry seem to prefer their own complexion to that of the extremely fair Germans and of dark-hued Africans; their darker hair and eyes to the blond hair and blue eyes of Germans; their noses to those of the hooked-nosed Persians or flat-nosed Africans. In view of the Greco-Roman aesthetic criteria, there was nothing unusual about the inclusion of color in judgments of beauty.[57] In short, like other people white and black, in their expressions of aesthetic preference the Greeks and Romans used their own physical traits as a yardstick. It is often overlooked, however, that there were whites as well as blacks who did not measure up to the Greco-Roman norm image. This omission in some modern interpretations results in an emphasis on blackness that distorts the classical view of the Ethiopians' color.

Particularly important in an assessment of the Greco-Roman reaction to the color black is the fact that in predominantly white societies there were those who emphasized the subjectivity of their criteria, others who extolled the beauty of blackness, and still others with preferences for blacks who had no hesitancy in saying so. Herodotus, the first European to express an opinion about the physical appearance of Ethiopians, described them as the most handsome of all men.[58] A poem of Philodemus to a certain Philaenion, short, black, with hair more curled than parsley and skin more tender than down, concludes: "May I love such a Philaenion, golden Cypris, until I find another more perfect."[59] Asclepiades praises the beauty of one Didyme: "Gazing at her beauty I melt like wax before the fire. And if she is black, what difference to me? So are coals, but when we light them, they shine like rose-buds."[60] Theocritus reminds those who call his Bombyca sunburned that to him she is honey-brown and charming and adds that violets and hyacinths are dark but are the first flowers chosen for nosegays.[61] Terence, perhaps of Negroid extraction, was freed by his master, according to Suetonius, because of his talent and his good looks: he was *fuscus* (dark).[62] Vergil explained his preference for a dark Amyntas (*fuscus*) by saying that violets and hyacinths are dark (*nigra*) and warned the fair Alexis (*candidus*) not to have too much faith in his color, for white privets fall but dark (*nigra*) hyacinths are picked.[63] Ovid's Sappho tells Phaon that she is not fair but reminds him that Andromeda, dark (*fusca*) with the hue of her native Ethiopia, captivated Perseus by her beauty.[64] Martial writes that, though he was sought by a girl whiter than a washed swan, than silver, snow, lily, or privet, he pursued a girl blacker than an ant, pitch, jawdaw, or cicada.[65]

One poem in praise of blackness, because it brings together several relevant themes, merits detailed analysis. The sixth-century poet Luxorius paid a tribute to Olympius, a famous black animal fighter, a Hercules in strength and a favorite of the people, which reads in part:

> O wonderful, O bold, O swift, O spirited O always ready! Not at all does your swarthy body harm you because of its blackness. So did nature create black precious ebony. So does the purple deeply placed in the tiny murex gleam, so do violets of deepest shade bloom in the soft grass, so does a certain grace set off gems of somber hue, so does the huge elephant please because of its dusky limbs, so do black Indian incense and pepper give pleasure. Finally, you are as beautiful in the great

love the people bear you as another man, handsome without strength, is ugly.[66]

Vergil's rejection of the prevailing aesthetic standard had included only violets and hyacinths as examples of dark beauty. The later poet retained Vergil's dark violets but, in order to emphasize the natural beauty of Ethiopian blackness, added more—precious luxury goods highly prized in antiquity. Luxorius, however, was not only writing of black physical beauty but was expressing another important idea: excellence is found among all men, whatever their race. Menander had said that natural bent, not race, determines nobility;[67] Agatharchides, that success in battle depends not upon color but upon courage and military science.[68] Similarly, for Luxorius, it was Olympius' strength and skill in the amphitheater that mattered. There is nothing in this tribute to justify a view that the references to color in the poem are pejorative. At the end of the classical period Luxorius, in an extravagant but still serious fashion, was using an ancient symbolism—black in a society with a somatic norm image of white—to emphasize the inconsequence of color in evaluating men.

What the majority of the people of Carthage thought about Olympius' intrinsic worth is suggested by Luxorius' epitaph to him:

Animal fighter who brought us great joy and often delighted us with your skill against the wild beasts—quick, pleasant, most brave, daring—who, as a boy that had not yet reached the age of young men, used to perform all feats with mature effort, who gave to others the privilege of winning with you, although you could give great pleasure to the spectators and win acclaim by yourself—so great were the rewards of your remarkable physique that after your death your companions are still awed by you and praise you.

Alas, now this tomb contains you carried off so unexpectedly by envious death, you whom the walls and towers of Carthage could not bear when you triumphed in the arena. But you lose nothing among the shades because of this bitter death. The fame of your glory will live everlastingly after you, and Carthage will always say your name![69]

A tribute by Luxorius to another invincible black athlete also refers indirectly to the champion's color, but only to praise him in glowing terms. Associating a famed black charioteer with mythological greats, Luxorius writes that he has the swiftness of Aeolus and Zephyrus; the color of Night, his mother, and of Memnon, but that unlike the great ally of the Trojans he will not meet death at the hands of Achilles.[70]

Thus "white" was for many in the ancient world a basic element in the somatic norm image, as it has usually been in predominantly white societies. The number of implied or expressed preferences in classical literature for white beauty exceeds slightly those for black or dark beauty. About this there is nothing strange. But what is unusual was the number of those in the Greco-Roman world who rejected the norm of whiteness and openly stated their rejection. As far as the Greeks and Romans were concerned, it seems the matter was basically one of individual preference. As Propertius observed, a tender beauty, white or dark, attracts,[71] and, as we have seen, the dark were inclusive—from *fuscae* to *nigerrimae*.

Art and the somatic norm image

A valuable source of information on attitudes toward the physical appearance of blacks is the copious evidence of art. Works of artists from Egyptian to Roman times confirm in a most striking manner written evidence of interracial mixture[72] and provide convincing testimony that the white somatic norm image was not always observed. These artists demonstrate clearly that some scholars have read nonexistent anti-black sentiment into Greco-Roman preferences which in fact merely reflected the prevailing norms, and were no more "racist" than the preferences of blacks for their ideals of beauty. Ancient artists have not left a record of their own feelings about the Negroes who served as their models. Suggestions as to their views, however, have not been lacking. Modern opinions have often been based on an examination of small samples because only recently has an extensive gallery of Negroes in art of the ancient world become available for study. We need a fresh look at modern interpretations of the ancient evidence.

Some scholars have seen an aesthetic antipathy to the Negro among ancient artists: C. T. Seltman stresses the appeal of the ugliness of Negroes;[73] W. N. Bates concludes that on Greek vases as a

rule the Negro is most absurdly drawn;[74] Martin Robertson observes
that Memnon was represented as white because of a Greek aversion
to Negroid features;[75] and others have seen primarily caricature or
the comic in ancient portrayals of blacks.[76] Some Negroes, but far
from the majority, appear in scenes that may rightly be classified as
comic or caricatural—a fourth-century B.C. Negroid Nike and Heracles from Cyrenaica (fig. 42), for example, or blacks in Kabeirion
episodes such as a Negroid Circe and Odysseus on a skyphos in the
British Museum (fig. 43). In some cases, a belief in the supposed
apotropaic charm of Negroes may have also been a factor, but some
critics have seen apotropaic, grotesque, and comic where none existed. Still there is no reason to conclude that classical artists who
depicted blacks in comic or satirical scenes were motivated by color
prejudice. Whites of many races—even gods and heroes—appeared
in comic or satirical scenes. Why should blacks have been excluded? If Negroes had been depicted only as comic or grotesque, or
if satirical scenes had been the rule and not the exception, there
might be some justification for a pejorative interpretation of the
Negro in classical art. In the absence of ancient evidence to support
such views, however, these suggestions must be regarded as the
opinions of modern critics, not of the artists themselves.

Classical artists, according to other interpretations, worked from
Negro models for no such motives as those cited above, but for
many of the same reasons as they selected whites, and often with
remarkable success. The Negroid Spinario (Boy Pulling Out a
Thorn) from Priene (fig. 44), which some have regarded as comic,[77]
R. A. Higgins has described as a "creation of unusual charm" and
"transformed by the coroplast into a human document, a sympathetic study of a racial type."[78] The vitality of the tiny Hellenistic
bronze head of a Negro in Florence was one of the qualities that
Herbert Read had in mind when he referred to the piece as "a great
work of art, even the greatest work of art in the world."[79] The terracotta of the sleeping emaciated boy in the Ashmolean (fig. 45),[80] according to A. J. Evans, "for life-like realism and true pathos is probably without a rival amongst Greek terra-cottas."[81] D. G. Mitten
ranks the Hellenistic bust of a Negro youth in Providence with "the
Pergamene Gauls as one of the most penetrating depictions of hos-

tile or captive ethnic types achieved by Hellenistic artists."[82] Deschamps finds in the blacks of classical art an astonishing diversity
and vividness, and a grace that bespeaks an absence of prejudice.[83]
A common view is that the treatment of blacks was in general sympathetic and that their continued popularity among the Greeks and
Romans was motivated by the artistic challenge of the physical
types, an impulse to realism, and pure aesthetic delight.[84]

Of the various foreign populations in the classical world, the
Negro attracted artists over a longer period of time than any other
alien type—long after the initial excitement and curiosity about a
novel element in the population had abated. One of the reasons was
aesthetic. In his rejection of conventional explanations of blacks in
Greek art, J. D. Beazley emphasizes the aesthetic attractiveness of
the Negro: "The black man gets in not because he has strong pro-
phylactic properties, nor because he is more addicted to wine, or
perfume, than the white man, nor because there were both per-
fumes and black men in Egypt, but because it seemed a crime not to
make negroes when you had that magnificent black glaze."[85] Aesthetic quality seems also to be the basis of Henri Metzger's observation that the black man had an uncontestable attraction for Greek
artists.[86] The features of the Negro presented a challenge to the skill
of the artist to represent, by texture and paint, the black man and
especially his hair. Jenifer Neils has pointed out that the painters of
the "Negro alabastra" (fig. 46) were particularly successful in delin-
eating the Negro's features by using black outline drawing on a
white ground, effectively representing the woolly hair by black dots,
reminiscent of the plastic points of head-vases, and contrasting the
black skin with the white ground.[87] The problem of painting blacks
on a black background was effectively met by the Niobid Painter's
depiction of Cepheus' Ethiopian attendants, with their mass of
woolly hair strikingly rendered in white.[88]

In addition, the presence of different Negroid and mixed types in
their midst presented opportunities for a diversity in physical types,
black-white contrasts, and artistic experimentation. Egyptian artists
were the first to make effective contrasts of blacks and whites—a
motif frequently employed in portraying pharaonic triumphs over
Negroes and Asiatics.[89] We may note further the varied concepts of

Negroid types in illustrations of the Andromeda and Busiris legends, the effective contrast of blacks and whites in the plastic head-
vases, and in the Herculaneum frescoes of the Isiac worship.[90]
When motifs "in white" such as the Boy Blowing a Fire (fig. 47), the
Spinario, or Eros had run their course, resourceful artists varied
traditional themes by turning for models to "pure" Negroes or mulattoes.[91]

The attitude of ancient artists toward their models is a matter that
must be based on a careful examination of the ancient works themselves. Regardless of the varied interpretations of modern scholars,
it is difficult to deny that the artists found in their Negro models interesting, if not in some instances aesthetically attractive, examples
of non-Greek and non-Roman types. In discussing the image of the
Negro in European art of a much later period, D. B. Davis has
pointed out that, in spite of the esteem of poets and painters for fair
complexions, Sir Thomas Browne, Sir Joshua Reynolds, and Lord
Kames considered standards of beauty a matter of custom, and the
"Europeans were by no means blind to the physical beauty of Negroes."[92] Davis in this observation is describing circumstances not
unlike those in which the classical image of blacks developed. We
do not know how many Greeks and Romans accepted the somatic
norm image of whiteness, stated or implied in some authors, but in
assessing the overall ancient view it is important not to overlook the
rejection of such a criterion as attested by the iconographical evidence for substantial racial mixture and by the aesthetic appeal of
Negroid types to classical artists.

Color symbolism

Among the Greeks and Romans, white was generally associated
with light, the day, with Olympus and victims sacrificed to the
higher gods, with good character and good omens; black with night
and darkness, with the Underworld, death, and chthonian deities,
with bad character and ill omens.[93] In this the Greeks and Romans
resembled people in general who, according to research on color
symbolism, have a basic tendency to equate blackness with evil and
white with goodness. Recent studies point out that there seems to be
a "widespread communality in feelings about black and white," that

among both Negroes and whites the color white tends to evoke a positive and black a negative reaction, and that both colors figure prominently in the areas of human experience concerned with religion and the supernatural.[94] C. N. Degler's observations on this subject underline the similarities between ancient and modern reactions to color: "It is surely more than a coincidence that in Africa and Asia as well as in Europe, black is associated with unpleasantness, disaster, or evil. Black undoubtedly evokes recollections of the night—that time when men, with their heavy dependence upon sight, are most helpless and in greatest danger. White, on the other hand, is the color of light, which emanates principally from the sun, which in turn is the source of warmth and the other conditions that support life. Night is not only dark, but cold and therefore a threat to life. Is it any wonder that white is seen everywhere as the symbol of success, virtue, purity, goodness, whereas black is associated with evil, dirt, fear, disaster, and sin?"[95]

It was obviously because of a deeply rooted tradition linking blackness with death and the Underworld that some writers of the early Roman Empire put dark-skinned peoples—Ethiopian, Egyptian, Garamantian—in ill-omened contexts. An Ethiopian was reported to have met troops of Cassius and Brutus as they were proceeding to battle.[96] At the time of Caligula's death, according to Suetonius, a nocturnal performance was in rehearsal in which scenes from the lower world were enacted by Egyptians and Ethiopians.[97] The events foreshadowing the death of Septimius Severus included the sight of an Ethiopian soldier carrying a garland of cypress boughs.[98] A metrical inscription from Hadrumetum (Sousse in southern Tunisia) deserves to be cited in full: "The dregs of the Garamantes have come up into our region and the black slave rejoices in his pitch-black body. If the voice issuing from his lips did not make him sound human, the grim ghost would be frightening upon sight. Hadrumetum, may ill-omened Tartarus carry off your monster for itself! The abode of Dis should have him as a guardian."[99]

Although the Greek and Roman association of the color black with death and the Underworld had in origin nothing to do with skin color, the introduction of dark-skinned peoples into such contexts was a natural development. Homer's and Vergil's underworlds were dark and murky; the god of the Underworld himself was often black;[100] and the ferryman Charon, son of Erebus and Night, was gloomy, grim, and terrible in his squalor.[101] The biographer of Septimius Severus was continuing this tradition when he noted the presence of an Ethiopian in the vicinity of the emperor on the eve of his departure to the dark Underworld whose presiding deity was black. Drawing on the language of Vergil's lower region, the Hadrumetum inscription is a *jeu d'esprit* on the common theme of the blackness of death and the Underworld. The pitch-black Garamantian (*piceo ... corpore ... niger*) of the Hadrumetum inscription is reminiscent of Vergil's grim warden Charon (*portitor ... horrendus*), guardian of black Tartarus (*nigra Tartara*); and the door of black Dis (*atri ianua Ditis*) in Vergil's Underworld[102] is echoed in the Hadrumetum inscription—the grim ghost (*horrida larva*) who should be the guardian of Dis. The intent is clear in both cases: mindful of widespread beliefs in the blackness of death and the nether realms, the biographer of Septimius Severus was aiming at complete coverage by including the Ethiopian in his catalogue of omens preceding the death of Septimius Severus—dreams, falling statues, black sacrificial victims; and the primary aim of the piece on the Garamantian was to echo traditional descriptions of the Underworld.

Interpretations that have seen a significant anti-black sentiment in the ancient association of Ethiopians with death and the Underworld are questionable. In the first place, the association seems to have been due primarily to the basic tendency of peoples, African Negroes included, to equate blackness and evil. Second, recent research in the social sciences has raised the question of whether individuals who react negatively to the color black also develop an antipathy toward dark-skinned people and suggests that, though such a reaction is in theory plausible, the evidence is far from conclusive.[103] It is doubtful, for example, that expressions such as blackball, blacklist, black mark, or black-hearted would in themselves have given rise to serious anti-Negro sentiments in the modern world in the absence of such phenomena as Negro slavery and colonialism.

In view of the overall attitude toward blacks in antiquity it is unlikely that the association of dark-skinned peoples with omens of evil in the early Roman Empire had an adverse impact on day-today reactions to blacks: the favorable image of Ethiopians had long been firmly established, and the unbiased environmental explanation of racial differences had been deeply rooted since the fifth century B.C. At the same time that the notion linking dark-skinned people and omens of disasters was being circulated, proponents of the environment theory were setting forth unprejudiced explanations of physical differences; the ancient image of just Ethiopians was being reinforced; and Christian authors were developing a rich black-white imagery emphasizing the black man's membership in the Christian brotherhood.[104]

The Environment Theory of Racial Differences

Xenophanes' contrast of Thracians and Ethiopians and the juxtaposed Negroes and whites of the early janiform vases[105] suggest that the Greeks perhaps by the sixth century B.C. had begun to seek an explanation of the physical differences between the extremely fair and the very black. The view that the flora, fauna, and human inhabitants of a region and their manner of life are determined to a large extent by diversity of climatic, topographical, and hydrographical conditions first appears in the Hippocratic Corpus. The author of On Airs, Waters, and Places illustrates this theory by describing the effect of soil, water, climate, and exposure upon the physique, character, and institutions of the Egyptians and Scythians.[106] In observations on the differences between hot and cold countries, On Regimen suggests a comparison of the Libyan and the Pontic, and the races nearest each.[107] Polybius points out that environmental conditions explain not only the great divergence in character, feature, and color of peoples living in widely separated regions but also their different modes of life.[108] Although not mentioned specifically by name in the earliest statements of the environment theory, with the growth in knowledge of Africa during the Ptolemaic and Roman periods, Ethiopians together with Scythians came to be used frequently to illustrate the effects of environment.

Classical anthropology accounted for Negroid physical characteristics and the mores of black societies in the same way that it explained those of whites. Of the many examples, one will suffice.

According to Pliny, heat is responsible for the scorched complexion, curly beards and hair, and tall stature of the Ethiopians, and the mobility of climate explains their wisdom; moisture in the opposite region of the world accounts for the tall men of the north with their white frosty skin and straight, yellow hair, their fierceness resulting from the rigidity of the climate; a mix of fire and moisture in the middle region of the earth explains men of medium stature, with a blended complexion and with gentle customs and fertile intellects.[109] Blacks and whites living at the outer extremities of the world were not alone in following a primitive way of life. All men, including the Greek and Roman inhabitants of the ideal intermediate zone, were subject to the same laws of nature. The savage mode of life of the Cynaetheans, who committed more crimes than any other people in Greece, was related to the rugged, inclement, gloomy atmosphere of Arcadia. And, as Diodorus observed, in view of the vast climatic differences there was nothing unusual in the fact that Ethiopians and Scythians differed in so many respects from Greeks and Romans.[110]

The most frequently cited characteristics of Ethiopians were scorched complexions, frizzy or woolly hair, and (less often) flat noses and thick lips; of northerners, straight (red or yellow) hair, blue eyes, and pale white skin. From the Greek and Roman point of view, however, the most arresting characteristic of Ethiopians was their blackness; of northerners, their hair. Ethiopians were the people most frequently selected to illustrate blackness of color. Mention is made, for example, of a flower as dark as an Ethiopian's skin and of tanning the skin until it resembles an Ethiopian's.[111] "To wash an Ethiopian white" was a familiar proverb.[112] The hair and, especially in Roman descriptions, the hairstyle set northerners apart: Gallia Comata was so called because the natives for the most part let their hair grow long; Martial speaks of Sygambrians with hair twisted in a knot; Juvenal mentions a German with blue eyes and yellow knotted hair; and Tacitus says that the mark of the Suebi is to comb the hair back over the side of the face and to tie it low in a knot behind.[113] Seneca emphasized that there was in reality nothing unusual about the physical characteristics of different racial types: "Amongst his own people the colour of the Ethiopian is not notable, and amongst the Germans red hair gathered into a knot is not unseemly for a man. You are to count nothing odd or disgraceful for an individual which is a general characteristic of his nation."[114] In a discussion of man's racial and individual varieties, Pliny the Elder asked, "Who ever believed in the Ethiopians before actually seeing them?"[115] Similarly, Lucian said that an Ethiopian who denied the existence of white or yellow men would be properly rebuked for insisting that there were no men other than blacks.[116]

The Scythians and Ethiopians were selected as favorite illustrations of the environment theory because, as physical and geographical extremes, they provided dramatic examples of man's diversity. Following the example of the "anthropologists," Menander, the comic poet of the late fourth and early third century B.C., used Ethiopians and Scythians in an entirely different context. It makes no difference whether one is as physically different from a Greek as an Ethiopian or Scythian: it is merit, not race, that counts.[117] In this statement Menander was attacking the validity of birth as a criterion for judging an individual, but he was not suggesting, as some have argued, the existence of a special belief concerning the inferiority of the Ethiopian qua Ethiopian. In other words, Ethiopians and Scythians exemplified for Menander the broad scale of human faculties and potentialities. These northern and southern peoples, first used in geographical contrasts, appeared in Menander in a social and moral context and, later, were to figure prominently in a highly spiritual Christian imagery.[118]

Arnold Toynbee considered both the environment theory and the race theory of the geneses of civilization intellectually vulnerable, but he found the former more imaginative, more rational, more human, and, above all, unprejudiced and possessing none of the repulsiveness of the latter. The Greeks explained obvious physical differences, Toynbee added, "as being the effects of diverse environments upon a uniform Human Nature, instead of seeing in them the outward manifestations of a diversity that was somewhat intrinsic in Human Nature itself."[119] And, of great importance for the ancient view of blacks, classical "anthropologists," like writers from Homer to Quintus of Smyrna, developed no special theory concerning the inferiority of blacks—an approach that differed greatly from later Western outlooks, often deeply ingrained with racism in folklore, literature, and science.

Blacks in Daily Life

Nubians who left their country for Egypt or elsewhere in Mediterranean lands were obviously conspicuous because of their color:
they were blacks in predominantly white societies. Did the presence
of black aliens in their midst and other factors such as color symbolism or aesthetic preferences trigger emotional or negative reactions
in whites? How did blacks actually fare in their day-to-day contacts
with whites outside Nubia?

Occupational integration

Enslaved prisoners of war undoubtedly accounted for a substantial
portion of the black population in countries beyond Nubia. The numerous bronzes and terracottas of Negroes found in various parts of
the Greco-Roman world often tell the story of black captives and
slaves—soldiers, defiant prisoners of war, musicians, actors, pugi-
lists, servants, houseboys, and day laborers of different kinds.[120]
Some of these blacks, who apparently fell upon hard times, caught
the eye of sympathetic artists—like the half-starved boy depicted in
the Hellenistic terracotta mentioned above,[121] who had perhaps accompanied his father to Alexandria in search of employment; or the
lonely young musician in bronze from Chalon-sur-Saône (fig. 48),[122]
whose expression suggests that he was recalling memories of his
distant homeland. Others fared better, like the young man of Negroid descent whose marble head, perhaps from a columbarium in
Rome (fig. 49), has been interpreted as a funerary portrait of a slave
or prisoner of war who had achieved success in the imperial administration of the early empire.[123]

Not all blacks in Egypt or elsewhere, however, were slaves. Under
the influence of an idée fixe of blacks as the immutable equivalent
of slaves, historians have given little attention to the mobility and
dispersal of blacks who voluntarily migrated in search of a better
life. The advantages of cosmopolitan centers like Alexandria and
Rome were as attractive to enterprising blacks as to others, Greek,
Syrian, or Jew, who migrated for many reasons—educational, occupational, or personal. Economic factors that in modern times have
attracted Sudanese to Cairo and Alexandria seemed to have stimu-

lated northward migrations of Nubians in antiquity as well.[124] The political and economic conditions of the Napatan and Meroïtic Kingdoms of Kush would have encouraged the migration of a number of blacks to various parts of the Mediterranean world. Trade had always been an important factor in the Nubian economy; Nubians, especially from the upper classes, knew the value of an acquaintance with the language and culture of Mediterranean countries. Some Nubians lived abroad, therefore, to further their commercial interests; others went to Alexandria and Athens to study and in some instances perhaps returned to stay.

Slave or free, blacks found in alien lands a *carrière ouverte aux talents* available to them as to others. In spite of the Egyptians' view that their land was the one that really mattered, and that outsiders lacked something of humanity, once a foreigner came to live in Egypt, learned the language, and adopted Egyptian dress, he or she was accepted as one of "the people."[125] On this point Henri Frankfort has observed: "The talented and industrious were not frustrated by a rigid class distinction or by a colour bar."[126] In Egypt blacks had for centuries found a career in the army a means of achieving positions of security and prestige. Pinehas, who was perhaps of Kushite extraction, attained high rank in the pharaoh's army: he was one of the last viceroys of Kush in the reign of Ramesses XI (1113–1085 B.C.) and remained in Kush, probably as its independent ruler, after the Egyptian withdrawal about 1085 B.C.[127] Beginning with the late second century B.C., foreigners in Egypt seem to have been increasingly recruited for both the royal bodyguard and the citizen garrison in Alexandria. It is not unlikely that the large basalt head of a Negro, found in Egypt and now in the Greco-Roman Museum in Alexandria, was that of an officer in the Ptolemaic army about 80–50 B.C.[128] Sidonius mentions that Cleopatra's ships were filled with pitch-black soldiers.[129] In view of the long history of black warriors, it is not surprising that Ethiopians looked to military careers. It is not possible to determine precisely the extent to which the Ptolemies used Ethiopian soldiers. Marcel Launey, though noting that black Africans were included in the contingents of Hellenistic armies, believes that the Ptolemies were circumspect in their use of blacks, on the ground that they could expect little profit from undisciplined peoples.[130] The well-attested tradition of black warriors as auxiliaries among other Mediterranean peoples, however, suggests that Launey has underestimated the use of black troops by the Ptolemies.

The busts and heads of nameless blacks from the last centuries B.C. and early centuries A.D., found in various parts of the Greco-Roman world, were frequently portraits of individuals who had voluntarily left Nubia for homes abroad. The marble head of a Negro found in the Greek East, now in the Brooklyn Museum (fig. 50a-b), has been interpreted as that of a soldier or official in the administration of a Greek ruler or a member of the household of a prominent Greek of the second century B.C.[131] Such an interpretation may be correct, but the Negro may have been, just as plausibly, one of a number of well-to-do blacks from the Meroïtic Kingdom of Kush who had settled abroad and achieved success in any of the fields open to newcomers. Black diplomats, though not a large percentage of the population outside Nubia, have been almost entirely overlooked.[132] A life-sized marble bust of the first century, in the Museo Torlonia in Rome, may represent one of the Negro ambassadors engaged in diplomatic relations with Rome's southern neighbors in Egypt.[133] Some ambassadors probably remained in their foreign posts after the completion of their assignments because they enjoyed life abroad.[134]

The evidence for the daily life of blacks is particularly instructive for the Roman period in northwest Africa. Numerous dark- and black-skinned and Negroid peoples, as we have seen, lived along the southern fringes of what is now the Maghreb. Several Ethiopian peoples are also reported to have migrated northward, Strabo informing us, for example, that the Pharusii moved about freely and came as far north as Cirta (Constantine, Algeria). The Pharusii who came to Cirta traveled, according to Strabo, on horses whose bellies were fitted with skins containing water.[135] Another means of transportation between north and south employed by blacks was the camel: in a mosaic of the late second or third century from Thysdrus (El Djem, Tunisia), a black youth follows a camel (fig. 51),[136] while two blacks in a third-century mosaic from Thuburbo Maius (Henchir Kasbat, Tunisia) drive dromedaries loaded with baskets.[137]

Blacks and their descendants in northwest Africa earned their livelihood in seaports, town, and country. In a third-century mosaic depicting a marine scene, found at Uàdi ez Zgaìa (between Lepcis and Tripoli, Libya), a brownish man is shown rowing a boat while a black man pulls in a big fish.[138] One of several laborers on a large estate in the vicinity of Uthina (Oudna, Tunisia) was a Negro fowler (fig. 52) placing his snares in the branches of a tree.[139] A black cook prepares a meal over a fire in a hunting scene depicted in a mosaic from the end of the third century, found at Hippo Regius (Annaba, Algeria).[140] Of five servants bringing accessories for a banquet shown in a third-century mosaic from Carthage (fig. 53), there is one whose broad nose and curly hair point to a Negroid ancestry.[141] The Negro appearing in a second- or third-century mosaic found in a bath at Thamugadi (Timgad, Algeria) suggests that in northwest Africa, as elsewhere in the ancient world, Negroes were employed as bath attendants.[142]

The black Olympius, as the tribute of the poet Luxorius attests, was an idol in Carthage. That Olympius was not the only black animal fighter in northwest Africa is shown by a mosaic found at Thysdrus, the seat of one of the largest buildings in Roman north Africa, an amphitheater built for 45,000 spectators. A third-century mosaic has preserved a vivid picture of five men, one unmistakably Negroid, drinking and talking, perhaps on the eve of their appearance in the amphitheater.[143] Another mosaic, also from Thysdrus, shows a black attendant making a tame panther drink.[144] A black wrestler (fig. 54) and a gladiator of black-white extraction are known from third-century works, the former appearing in a mosaic found at Thaenae (Henchir Thina, Tunisia) and the latter, a terracotta statue from Carthage.[145] North African blacks apparently developed considerable experience in the management and handling of horses. A black man stands beside one of the more than eighty race horses that make up a huge mosaic from a villa near Carthage.[146] Four horses and their grooms, one black, are the subject of a third-century mosaic from Hadrumetum (Sousse, Tunisia).[147] Black grooms (fig. 55) appear at the entrance of stables in a sixth- or seventh-century circus scene from Capsa (Gafsa, Tunisia).[148] It is not known whether the black charioteer celebrated in a poem by Luxorius was a groom in his youth.[149] It is reasonable to suggest, however, that some grooms like those in the mosaics cited above became charioteers in their later careers and achieved success, if not the reputation of Luxorius' hero.

C. Julius Serenus, of unmistakable black-white extraction, had apparently attained a degree of financial prosperity, suggested by the scenes seemingly commissioned for a mosaic, found at Thaenae, dating from the third or fourth century (fig. 56). In separate panels Serenus and Numitoria Saturnina, who is white, are portrayed taking part in their own funeral banquet: each in a semi-reclining position, holding a golden goblet in the right hand. Three Cupids appear in each panel, one filling a basket with flowers, a second carrying flowers to the reclining spouse, and the third playing a cithara.[150] Although nothing else is known of the life of C. Julius Serenus, his career may have been somewhat similar to that of a landowner from Mactaris (Mactar, Tunisia), born of humble parents, who by careful attention to the land and by his industry as a foreman at harvest time acquired a fortune and was honored with a seat in the local senate.[151]

Although there is no record of separate Ethiopian *numeri* (ethnic units named after the region of recruitment), the Roman imperial armies included a number of Ethiopian or mixed black-white recruits such as those who served in the elite Moorish cavalry in Dacia, in the *numerus Maurorum* of Septimius Severus' army in Britain, and perhaps in Constantine's siege of Verona and the battle of the Mulvian bridge.[152] In view of the African connections of Septimius Severus, it is not unlikely that the emperor recruited other blacks from northwest Africa, like the Negroid soldier in the scene on a third-century sarcophagus, perhaps a member of Septimius Severus' elite bodyguard.[153]

Cultural assimilation

The name of Hellene, according to the Athenian orator Isocrates, should be applied to persons sharing in the culture, rather than the ancestry, of the Greeks.[154] Measured by such a criterion, blacks had to be counted among those who had assimilated, in varying degrees, Greek culture. The Meroïtes apparently regarded a knowledge of

Greek as an indispensable tool for many purposes. Remains of a column from Meroë with the Greek alphabet written around it suggest that some Meroïtic children received instruction in the rudiments of Greek.[155] The Ethiopian king Ergamenes, according to Diodorus, had a Greek education and studied Greek philosophy.[156] Where Ergamenes studied is not known, but Alexandria was a likely center for the education of the children of well-to-do Meroïtes. The Negro boy in bronze (in Boston) from the Hellenistic period was perhaps the portrait of an aristocratic lad who had left the south to study in Alexandria.[157] The eunuch, an official of the Ethiopian queen, who was reading a roll of Isaiah when he met Philip apparently read Greek, and, perhaps, Hebrew.[158] An Ethiopian, Maximus the decurion as he called himself in an acrostical introduction of a hymn to Mandulis, a Nubian deity associated with Isis, was one of the soldiers and pilgrims whose inscriptions have been found at a temple in the Roman garrison town of Talmis (Kalabsha) in Nubia. Inspired by the blessed loneliness of the spot, Maximus, in his hymn, written at some time between the end of the first and third centuries, declared that Mandulis in his splendor had come down from Olympus and exhorted him to compose his tribute in sweet Hellenic verse instead of in the barbarisms of the Ethiopian tongue.[159]

Reported among the disciples of Aristippus, a Cyrenaic philosopher, was a certain Aethiops, and included in a list of the distinguished followers of Epicurus (341–270 B.C.) were two from Alexandria named Ptolemaeus, otherwise unknown, one black, the other white.[160] An elderly Negroid man appearing on a fragment of a third-century sarcophagus (fig. 57) has been interpreted as one of the philosopher types popular on the sarcophagi of the muses in that century.[161] Much better known are the careers of two other Africans, perhaps of Negroid descent, the well-known Roman playwright Terence (ca. 190–159 B.C.), an ex-slave from Carthage, who received the patronage of the Scipionic circle,[162] and Juba II (died ca. 23 A.D.), King of Mauretania (fig. 58), a man of learning who strove to introduce Greek and Roman culture into his African kingdom.[163] Among Juba's many works (now lost), written in Greek, were a history of Rome, books on Libya and Assyria, and treatises on drama, painting, and plants. A Negro, known only as Memnon, was considered one of the most talented disciples of Herodes Atticus, the celebrated sophist and patron of the arts in the second century.[164]

"The making of a mental note of differences between the self and others," C. N. Degler has pointed out, "even when the other is a darker color, is only a first step in making social distinctions. It may be the only step taken, in which case there are no measurable social consequences, for what goes on in a human head without affecting behavior is not socially important."[165] The careers of Negroes and other dark-skinned peoples in predominantly white societies illustrate another notable aspect of the racial pattern in antiquity: blacks suffered no detrimental distinctions that excluded them from opportunities—occupational, economic, or cultural—available to other newcomers in alien lands.

Racial mixture

In the modern world the attitude of whites toward racial mixing has often been regarded as a crucial criterion of the white man's view of blacks. A significant commentary on the attitude toward black-white racial mixture is found in classical mythology: the presence of black gods or heroes and their interracial amours presented no embarrassment and evoked no apologies from poets or artists. Richard Carden has suggested that Zeus, called Ethiopian by the inhabitants of Chios, may have been the black- or dark-faced stranger in the *Inachus* of Sophocles (ca. 496–406 B.C.) and may have appeared as a Negro in the dramatist's satyr-play.[166] Epaphus, the child that Io, the daughter of the primeval king of Argos, bore Zeus, was described by Aeschylus (ca. 525–456 B.C.) as black and was said by Hesiod (fl. ca. 700 B.C.) to have been the ancestor of the Libyans and Ethiopians.[167] In the *Suppliants* of Aeschylus, the daughters of Danaus were black and smitten by the sun, seven of them, according to a later version of the legend, born to Danaus by an Ethiopian woman.[168] The Egyptian sojourn of the descendants of Io left, in the words of Aubrey Diller, "a smear of foreign ancestry in the lineage of the Argive and Dorian kings that had to be either ignored or made the best of. It was never denied."[169] Delphos, the eponymous founder of Delphi, the son of Poseidon or Apollo and a woman, several variants of whose name mean the Black Woman, is the most likely identification for the Negro appearing on the coinage of Athens at the end of the sixth century B.C. and of Delphi in the fifth.[170] Ovid suggests that a black lover of Aurora was the father of Memnon.[171] Perseus, the son of Zeus by Danaë, married the dark-skinned Andromeda, whose father, king of the Ethiopians, was a mulatto (fig. 59), at least in the eyes of a vase painter in the mid-fifth century B.C.[172] In an "Ethiopian romance," Heliodorus' *Aethiopica*, a descendant of Achilles was enamored of a girl whose parentage was unknown to both, because her mother had exposed her at birth to avoid being charged with adultery for having borne a white child: the eventual discovery that her parents were the black king and queen of Ethiopia did not matter to her Greek hero. Nothing in the recital of these legends indicates that the racial mixture was considered strange or undesirable.

The unknown prince of a royal family and his Negro wife are the earliest known examples (ca. 2600 B.C.) of an interracial couple in Egypt.[173] Other ladies of pharaonic courts were at times Nubian, a striking example being Queen Tiy, the chief wife of Amenophis III.[174] Negro mercenaries, like those in Gebelein, found wives in Egypt, and the rebellious soldiers of Psamtik I, according to Herodotus, had no hesitancy about marrying Ethiopian women.[175] The "Cushite woman" whom Moses married was, according to Josephus, Tharbis, daughter of the Ethiopian king.[176] (Verdi's Aida, one notes, was not the first Ethiopian princess to attract an admirer from Egypt.) The daughter of the dark-skinned Terence is said to have married a Roman knight.[177] King Juba II of Mauretania, was married first to Cleopatra Selene, the daughter of Antony and Cleopatra, and later to Glaphyra, the daughter of Archelaus, king of Cappadocia. The genealogies of the many obviously mixed black-white types portrayed in Egyptian, Hellenistic, and Roman art seldom come to light. Little is known about the several dark and black beauties praised in Greek and Latin poetry: one point, however, is certain—there is no question about their color, from the blackness of Asclepiades' Didyme to the pitch-blackness of Martial's unnamed lady.[178] Pompeiian graffiti indicate that black women were not unknown in the Campanian demimonde.[179]

Racial mixture of blacks and whites was a topic mentioned by several Greek and Roman authors. Aristotle was the first to call attention to the transmission of physical characteristics of descendants of black-white crosses.[180] Plutarch related a story about a Greek women whose black baby caused her to be accused of adultery, although an investigation of her lineage revealed that she was the great-granddaughter of an Ethiopian.[181] Martial in an epigram on adultery mentions black children among the offspring, and Juvenal implies that mulattoes would be more common were it not for the practice of abortion.[182] In the early Roman Empire an apparently popular theory of "maternal impression" was developed to explain the color of children unlike their mother's. Jerome mentioned Quintilian's argument that a matron charged with adultery had given birth to an Ethiopian as a result of maternal impression.[183] The black Ethiopian queen Persinna in the *Aethiopica* of Heliodorus, upon discovering that she had given birth to a white daughter, recalled that at the time of conception she was looking at a picture depicting Perseus' rescue of Andromeda.[184]

Writers who had occasion to refer to interracial marriages or to mention black-white racial mixture, either as illustrations of the transmission of inherited physical characteristics, as evidence of adultery, or for any other reason, developed no theories of "white purity" and included nothing resembling later strictures on racial mixture. Neither the biblical account of Moses' marriage to a Kushite nor that of Josephus condemns the union.[185] The reasons for the anger of Miriam and Aaron as given in the Old Testament are not expressly stated, but, as Ronald Sanders has pointed out, the issue was apparently not color prejudice, and "Whatever Miriam and Aaron may feel, God and Moses are certainly on the side of the Ethiopian."[186] Josephus in his version does not suggest that there was anything unusual about the overture of the Ethiopian princess or about Moses' acceptance of her proposal. And, as we shall see, the Moses-Ethiopian marriage was to become for the early Christians a meaningful symbol in the interpretation of Christianity's mission.

Realistic portrayals of mulattoes and of mixed black-white types in ancient art vividly illustrate various steps in the so-called disappearance of Negroid physical traits—a process of "whitening out," frequently mentioned as a characteristic of Iberian-Caribbean societies—and provide dramatic confirmation of the racial mixture noted in ancient texts.[187] There is little doubt that many blacks were physically assimilated into the predominantly white population of the Mediterranean world, in which there were no institutional barriers or social pressures against black-white unions. In antiquity, then, black-white sexual relations were never the cause of great emotional crises. The general acceptance of miscegenation in the Maghreb, even in the best families, according to L. C. Brown, may have been one of several variables explaining North African indifference to color.[188] The Latin American attitude toward color, Hoetink has suggested, may have resulted from the "existence of a socioracial continuum in the Latin countries, which means that the white group has not consistently tried to evade racial mixing with contiguous color gradations."[189] The ancient pattern, similar in some respects to the Maghrebian and the Latin American attitude toward racial mixture, probably contributed to the absence of a pronounced color prejudice in antiquity.

Religion

The pronouncements and structure of organized religion are often important factors in the assessment of racial attitudes. Evidence on the views of blacks in the religions of the ancient world comes primarily from two areas, Isiac worship and especially Christianity.

Isiac worship

The worship of the goddess Isis, deeply rooted among Egyptians and Ethiopians, developed into a cult that spread from northeast Africa throughout the Greco-Roman world. Isis was worshiped by many peoples under a variety of names, but it was the Ethiopians and Egyptians who, according to Apuleius, called the deity by her true name, Queen Isis.[190] The island of Philae, at the head of the First Cataract, was especially sacred to the Ethiopians, who transported an image of the goddess to her shrine at Philae in an annual ceremony.[191] Blacks frequently played an influential role in the spread of the Isiac rituals, but Ethiopian influence was perhaps most pervasive at Philae, because it was within reach of large numbers of Ethiopians, and the cult flourished there after the spread of Christianity elsewhere in the region.[192] Philae, the Mecca or Jerusalem of Isiac worship, attracted worshipers of many classes and nationalities who welcomed the opportunity to express devotion to the "Queen of the Southern Peoples" at one of her most sacred shrines.[193]

Some of the most vivid examples of Ethiopian participation in the Isiac cult come not from Africa, but from Italy. A fresco from Herculaneum depicts preparations for the departure of a procession of Isiac cultists, black and white, men and women (fig. 60). Of the blacks, one, holding a sistrum, stands at the front of a temple door beside a central figure, flanked on the other side by a priestess, also shaking a sistrum. A second black is a choirmaster seemingly directing a chorus of the faithful of both sexes, turned toward him. In the foreground are two other blacks, one seated at the extreme right playing a flute, the other standing at the extreme left, brandishing a sistrum. The shoulders and arms of three of the blacks are bare, their robes knotted at the waist, extending only from below the armpits, while the black flutist is dressed like the white cultists with the upper part of his body covered by his robe.[194] In a companion fresco from Herculaneum (fig. 61) the central figure, a black man, executes a dance, with the eyes of most worshipers focused upon him. The dancer is naked except for a loincloth; his head has a leafy headdress reminiscent of the feathered headpiece of the god Bes; and his body, arms, and forehead seem to be covered with strokes of paint. In this tableau other blacks appear, one kneeling as he claps his hands, another playing a flute, and a third holding a sistrum, and all with arms and shoulders bare like the blacks in the companion fresco. In the foreground of each fresco two ibises walk about—a detail recalling the Nilotic origin of the cult, probably important for the authenticity of the ritual.[195] Another view of an Isiac ritual appears in a scene on a marble relief of the early second century, at one time part of a sarcophagus on the Via Appia near Ariccia. In the courtyard of an Isiac temple a ceremony is in progress in which violent dancing, involving bending the knees and tossing back the head, is accompanied by music provided by castanets and what seem to be double flutes. A frenzied audience joins in the ritual by clapping as the dancers and musicians, some pronouncedly Ne-

groid, pay homage to the goddess, whose African homeland is recalled by the ibises, palm tree, and god Bes included in the temple
decoration.[196]

Ethiopians were obviously welcomed as priests and cultists by
Isis followers in Greece, Italy, and other centers of the cult, where
their expert ritualistic knowledge and their authentic dances and
music lent a note of genuineness to the ceremonies. A bond united
black and white in the worship of a goddess who, in the words of
R. E. Witt, "came to win the unswerving love and loyalty of countless men and women of every rank . . . she did not allow room . . .
for any prudery about sex, or racial discrimination and segregation
according to the colour of one's skin."[197] In short, strangers though
Ethiopians may have been when they reached foreign lands, the re-
ception of fellow cultists gave them a spiritual security in their
adopted countries. A black man, far from his homeland, may have
been like Apuleius' Lucius, "a stranger to the temple but at home in
the [Isiac] faith."[198]

Christianity

The strong bond that had united blacks and whites in the common
worship of Isis was reinforced by Christianity. Like the Isiac cult,
Christianity swept racial distinctions aside. Scythians and especially Ethiopians figured prominently in the imagery and basic pronouncements of the early Christian credo. Statements of the environment theory had frequently cited Scythians and Ethiopians as
examples of man's physical diversity. Menander had employed the
Ethiopian-Scythian formula to express his views of the equality of
men. When Origen declared that all whom God created He created
equal and alike, whether they were born among the Hebrews,
Greeks, Ethiopians, Scythians or Taurians,[199] he was adapting a
formula well known in classical thought which left no doubt as to
its meaning and comprehensiveness. Toward the end of the sixth
century, Venantius Fortunatus, Bishop of Poitiers, used the same
Ethiopian-Scythian antithesis to dramatize the successes of apostolic
endeavors: Paul, by penetrating Scythian snows, mitigated the cold
of the north by the warm glow of his message, and by his words
Matthew tempered the Ethiopian heat and caused living rivers to

flow in the parched deserts of the south.[200] Such imagery underscored the ecumenical mission of Christianity: all peoples—from
the blackest to the whitest at the very ends of the earth—were summoned to salvation.

Early Christian writers referred to Ethiopians and blackness primarily in two major contexts, demonological and exegetical. From
the Greek and Roman point of view, we have seen, the unusual and
distinctive physical characteristic of Ethiopians was their blackness. And the color black, for the Greeks and Romans as for other
peoples, evoked a negative, and white a positive image. The demonological references to Ethiopians and blackness, covering a very
limited area, were obviously related to the Greco-Roman association of black with evil and the Underworld. In apocryphal and patristic literature black was the color of the devil and of some
demons who tempted early Christians or troubled them in visions
and dreams.[201] As early as the *Epistle of Barnabas* (ca. 70–100 A.D.)
the devil was called the Black One; and the way of the Black One
was described as crooked and full of curses because it was the way
of eternal death with punishment where one finds the things that
destroy men's souls.[202] In an encounter with Melania the Younger,
the devil disguised himself as a young black man.[203] The devil is
black, according to Didymus the Blind, because he fell from the
splendor and virtue and spiritual whiteness that only those who
have been "whitened" by God can possess.[204]

In the vision of saints and monks, demons at times assumed the
shape of "Ethiopians." Whether these Ethiopians, incarnations of
evil and temptation, sometimes repulsive and unsightly, appeared
as women, little boys, or giants,[205] the emphasis was on the color
black—a contrast between the blackness of evil and the light of
God. Hues of darkness other than Ethiopian appeared in this symbolism. The devil, for example, was depicted as Egyptian; and
demons, as crows or merely black.[206] A key to the emphasis on
color, however, appears especially in the description of a female
demon in the *Acts of Peter* (ca. 150–200 A.D.), as " 'most Ethiopian'
(*Ethiopissimam*), not Egyptian, but altogether black," phraseology
reminiscent of the gradations of color found in classical descriptions of Ethiopians, Indians, Egyptians, and other dark peoples.[207]
As J. M. Courtès has pointed out, "The concept of the black hardly

goes beyond that of skin coloration, which seems to be the only racial characteristic taken into account by Christian writers . . . blackness [is regarded] simply as the darkest of various shades of color
found among the peoples of the Mediterranean Basin and the
East."[208] Also related perhaps to the emphasis on color and the absence of any similarity to real Ethiopians is the fact that later medieval iconography, in spite of the black and Ethiopian apparitions of
apocryphal and patristic literature, portrayed so few demons with
Negroid features.[209]

The symbolism of black demons, like the association of black
with death and ill omens in the secular sphere, does not seem to
have had a negative effect on the generally favorable view of blacks
dating back to the Homeric poems,[210] or to have given rise to a serious anti-black sentiment. And, with respect to fundamental Christian beliefs, exegetical interpretations of scriptural Ethiopians,
much broader in scope than the limited demonological references,
set forth a coherent body of doctrine in which Ethiopians in fact
became an important symbol of Christianity's ecumenical mission.
Building on classical color usages, the Christian writers developed
an exegesis and a black-white imagery in which Ethiopians illustrated the meaning of the Scriptures for *all* men. In short, antiquity
as a whole was able to overcome whatever potential for serious
anti-black sentiment there may be in color symbolism.

The pioneer in the use of an Ethiopian symbolism was Origen,
who became the model for later patristic treatment of Ethiopian
themes and who shaped the tradition of this type of exegesis. Origen's choice of a black-white imagery may have been inspired in
part by his firsthand acquaintance with blacks in the motley population of Alexandria, a daily reminder of the many Ethiopians at the
southern periphery of the world who had figured prominently in
classical imagery. By adapting this symbolism and by relying on familiar patterns of thought, Origen and others after him realized that
they could interpret scriptural references more meaningfully and
could explicate their message more convincingly.

The essential spirit of Origen's Ethiopian interpretations appears
in his commentaries on the Song of Songs, in which he also includes observations on other important scriptural references to
Ethiopians.[211] The superficial meaning of the bride's words, "I am

black and beautiful" (1:5 LXX),[212] according to Origen, is that the bride is black in complexion, but, having both natural beauty and inward beauty acquired by practice, she should not be reproached.[213] Statements of preference as to physical beauty had not been uncommon in classical literature. Origen's observations on "black and beautiful" were reminiscent of those Greeks and Romans who rejected the ethnocentric yardstick of the majority and considered blacks naturally beautiful. The bride's words, Origen explains further, also have a mystical meaning. Representing the church gathered from among the Gentiles, the bride is replying to the daughters of an earthly Jerusalem who vilify her because of her ignoble birth. Though not descended from famous men, the bride has, she says, a beauty deriving from the Image and Word of God.[214] In the fifth century B.C. Antiphon the Sophist, in arguing for the oneness of Greeks and barbarians, had attacked the practice of revering those born of noble fathers and of failing to honor those of ignoble origin.[215]

The mystery of the church arising from the Gentiles and calling itself black and beautiful, Origen points out, is adumbrated elsewhere in the Scriptures. The marriage of Moses to a black Ethiopian woman is interpreted as a symbolic union of the spiritual law (Moses) and the church (the Ethiopian woman)—a foreshadowing of the universal church.[216] Another adumbration of this mystery of the church, according to Origen, was the visit of the Queen of Sheba to Solomon. In fulfillment of her type, the queen who came from the south, Ethiopia, the church comes from the Gentiles to hear the wisdom of the true Solomon and true peacelover Jesus Christ.[217] By saying that the queen came from the ends of the earth, and that she was called the queen of the south because Ethiopia lies in the southern regions, Origen recalls Homer's Ethiopians, the most distant of men.

In support of his view that Ethiopians represented the church of the Gentiles, Origen cited other scriptural passages: a line from a hymn of praise, "Ethiopia shall stretch out her hand first to God";[218] Zephaniah's prophecy that "from beyond the rivers of Ethiopia . . . they shall bring sacrifices to me";[219] and the Ethiopian Ebed-melech's intervention on behalf of Jeremiah.[220] These three references suggest the precedence of Ethiopia, the people of the Gentiles, in approaching God. But an "Ethiopian" priority with respect to the divine was not at all a new concept: in his interpretation Origen was in part adapting a Greco-Roman view that Ethiopians were the first to honor the gods.[221]

In classical thought the blackness of the Ethiopian was only skin-deep. Blacks could have a soul as pure as the whitest of the whites: the queen of Meroë, in the Alexander Romance, cautioning the world conqueror about drawing conclusions from the Ethiopian's color, said "We are whiter in our souls than the whitest of you."[222] An epitaph of the third century, found at Antinoöpolis in Egypt, contrasted the black skin of a slave darkened by the rays of the sun and his soul blooming with white flowers.[223] In this tradition of outer blackness and inner whiteness Origen commented on another verse from the Song of Songs: "Look not upon me that I am dark, because the sun has looked down on me." Recalling the environment theory, Origen contrasts the natural blackness of Ethiopians caused by the sun with the blackness of the soul, which, unlike the Ethiopian's color transmitted by genetic inheritance, is acquired through neglect.[224] In the tradition of the Ethiopian-Scythian antithesis, Origen remarks that the visible sun darkens those to whom it comes close but does not burn those who are distant. The spiritual Sun of Justice, however, illuminates and brightens the upright in heart but looks askance at and blackens the disobedient.[225]

In images emphasizing the blackness of sin and the "Ethiopian" beauty of the converted, Origen shows the applicability of this black-white symbolism to all men: "We ask in what way is she black and in what way fair without whiteness. She has repented of her sins; conversion has bestowed beauty upon her and she is sung as 'beautiful' . . . if you repent, your soul will be 'black' because of your former sins, but because of your penitence your soul will have something of what I may call an Ethiopian beauty."[226] In his language of spiritual blackness and whiteness Origen's adaptation of the Greco-Roman black-white imagery is clear, but equally apparent is his indebtedness to classical themes of black-white contrasts.

Examples of Ethiopian symbolism, many showing the influence of Origen, are rather numerous in Christian writers of the fourth and fifth centuries; a few examples will suffice to give an idea of the range and the spirit of the Ethiopian theme. Christ came into the world, wrote Gregory of Nyssa, to make blacks white, not summoning to himself the just but calling to penitence sinners whom through baptism he made shine like heavenly bodies. This was what, according to Gregory, David saw in the heavenly city and caused him to marvel, for in the City of God "Gentiles become dwellers of the city; Babylonians, Jerusalemites; the prostitute, a virgin; Ethiopians, radiantly white, and Tyre, the heavenly city."[227] Ethiopians, in the interpretation of Cyril of Alexandria, are those whose dark minds are not yet illumined by divine light. They who kneel before Christ, however, are regarded as those of whom it has been written: "before Him shall the Ethiopians fall down" whereas those whose uncleanness is hard to wash out and who remain in their blackness will feast upon the heads of the dragons and will be exposed to the sword.[228] In commenting upon "Ye also, O Ethiopians, shall be slain by the sword," Jerome notes that those sunk in vice are called Ethiopians in accordance with the words of Jeremiah. If the Ethiopian changes his skin, in the conversion of the Ethiopians there is the hope that no one wishing to repent will be without salvation. This is why a soul stained with sin says "I am black" and later, washed and purged through penitence, is greeted, in the Song of Songs: "Who is she that cometh up having been made white?"[229]

Augustine's Ethiopian exegesis, like Origen's, may have been inspired in part by his firsthand experience with African blacks. In explicating a verse from the Psalms, Augustine states that under the name "Ethiopia" all nations were signified, a part representing the whole, and "properly by black men, for Ethiopians are black. Those are called to the faith who were black, just they, so that it may be said to them, 'Ye were sometimes darkness but now are ye light in the Lord.' They are indeed called black but let them not remain black, for out of these is made the church to whom it is said: 'Who is she that cometh up having been made white?' " For, concludes Augustine, what has been made out of the black maiden is what is said in "I am black and beautiful."[230] When Augustine declared that the catholic church was not to be limited to a particular region of the earth but would reach even the Ethiopians, the remotest and blackest of men, he was not only recalling Homer's distant Ethiopians, but he also had in mind perhaps those Ethiopians on the southernmost fringes of his own bishopric in northwest Africa.

The imagery of Ethiopians and their color was much more than a literary device: it was a dramatic means of presenting cardinal tenets of Christianity that were to be translated into practice. The Ethiopian eunuch, a high official of the queen of Ethiopia and in charge of all her treasure, was said to have been the first Gentile to receive from Philip the mystery of the divine Word.[231] It is not certain whether Philip's baptism of the Ethiopian was a straightforward record of actual events, suggested by hints in the Old Testament, or was included to illustrate the fulfillment of the promise of bearing witness "to the ends of the earth."[232] What is clear, however, is that for the readers of Acts the message was unequivocal: the Ethiopian man, as the eunuch was described, meant a black man and, in the minds of most, a Negro from the south of Egypt. The eunuch came to be admired as a model of the diligent reader of the Scriptures. John Chrysostom, for example, pointed to the eunuch as one who, though a barbarian without advantages, read the Scriptures in spite of other important matters occupying his attention.[233] Prepared for baptism by the reading of the prophet, the eunuch prefigured the peoples of the Gentiles, changed his skin, and, in the opinion of Jerome, provided an answer to Jeremiah's question, "Can the Ethiopian change his skin or the leopard his spots?"[234]

To Theodoret, as to many others, the eunuch was proof that "Ethiopia shall stretch out her hands to God."[235] And in fact Philip's baptism of the eunuch did foreshadow what was to be the practice of the church in the first centuries after Christ. Christianity was introduced into Axumite Ethiopia in the fourth century.[236] Ecclesiastical historians of the late fourth and fifth centuries reported that Ethiopians had been seen with monks in the Egyptian desert and that many of them excelled in virtue, thus fulfilling the words of the Scriptures.[237] In the sixth century there was an outburst of missionary activity in Nubia. Exactly when Nubia received its first black bishop is not known, but by the tenth century bishops, probably of local origin, occupied the episcopal seat at Faras (Pachoras) in

Lower Nubia. The unquestionably Negroid remains of one of these bishops, named Petros, were found in the cathedral at Faras, where his portrait was also preserved in a fresco.[238]

From northwest Africa came a dramatic application of Augustine's statement on the ecumenical mission of the church, which was to embrace the world's southernmost inhabitants, the Ethiopians.[239] An exchange of letters between a deacon of the church of Carthage and Fulgentius, Bishop of Ruspe, is concerned with the spiritual welfare of a black catechumen, Ethiopian in color, not yet whitened by the shining grace of Christ, from the most distant parts of a barbarous region where men are blackened by the sun.[240] This exchange of letters was vivid testimony that the vision of Augustine, "Aethiopia credet Deo,"[241] had become a reality in a distant region of northwest Africa.

But blacks were not simply to be humble converts. The lives of two men, one perhaps and the other certainly black, illustrate another aspect of the spirit of early Christianity. Menas (third-fourth century), sometimes portrayed as a Negro, was a national saint of Egypt. From the fifth to the seventh centuries the shrine of the Egyptian martyr west of Alexandria attracted pilgrims from Asia and Europe as well as from Africa, who returned to their homes with holy water or oil in small pottery flasks bearing the saint's name and effigy. On some of these ampullae, in a variant from the usual type, Menas is represented as a Negro (fig. 62), perhaps pointing to one tradition that the saint was of Nubian ancestry.[242] One of the most outstanding Desert Fathers was a tall, black Ethiopian, Abba Moses, whose fame spread far from the desert of Scete, where he acquired a reputation as a model of Christian virtue and humility, leaving some seventy disciples when he died at the age of seventy-five, at the end of the fourth or in the first years of the fifth century. According to an anonymous account of his life, Moses was everything to all, a model of the monastic life, an excellent teacher, a Fathers' Father.[243]

During the first six centuries of Christianity, blacks were summoned to salvation and were welcomed in the Christian brotherhood on the same terms as other converts. Philip's baptism of the Ethiopian was a landmark in the evangelization of the world.[244]

Origen and his exegetical disciples made it clear that all men, regardless of the color of their skin, were called to the faith, and in their interpretations they employed a deeply spiritualized black-white imagery. As late as the fifth and sixth centuries, Christian writers were still adhering to Origen's reading of the scriptural Ethiopians. The mid-fifth-century *Book of God's Promises and Predictions,* attributed to Quodvultdeus, an African bishop, chose Origen's Ethiopians to illustrate the prophetic truth of the Old Testament: the criticism of Jesus for associating with sinners and publicans had been foreshadowed by the critics of Moses for his marriage to the Ethiopian woman, and Christ had taken as his bride an Ethiopian, the church of the Nations, who had said, "I am black and beautiful, daughters of Jerusalem."[245] Philip's baptism of the Ethiopian was the subject of verses in which the north Italian poet Arator in the sixth century revived the salient components of imagery seen first in Origen—the marriage of Moses to the Ethiopian woman, the eternal bride of the church, which came, like the dark and beautiful maiden, from the burned regions of Ethiopia. The Ethiopian was still for Arator, as for the reader of Acts, a black man, and he continued to be a dramatic symbol of Christianity's catholic mission,[246] as he had been for the African Origen.

In spite of the association of blackness with ill omens, demons, the devil, and sin, there is in the extant records no stereotyped image of Ethiopians as the personification of demons or the devil, no fixed concept of blacks as evil or unworthy of conversion. On the contrary, the Ethiopian imagery dramatically emphasized the ecumenical character of Christianity and adumbrated the symbolism of the black wise man in the Adoration of the Magi. Nor is there any evidence that Ethiopians of the first centuries after Christ suffered in their day-to-day contacts with whites as a result of metaphorical associations of this symbolism. The reason is understandable: the Christian black-white symbolism, like the antecedent classical imagery of blackness and whiteness, was rooted in a Weltanschauung in which skin color did not give rise to a marked antipathy toward blacks and did not evoke negative reactions in the domain of social behavior. The early Christians did not alter the classical color symbolism or the teachings of the church to fit a preconceived notion of blacks as inferior, to rationalize the enslavement of blacks, or to sanction segregated worship. In sum, in the early church blacks found equality in both theory and practice.

This chapter has called attention to some important areas in which white-black relationships in antiquity differed from the racial patterns in a number of later societies. The differences are striking: in the ancient world there were prolonged black-white contacts, from an early date; first encounters with blacks frequently involved soldiers or mercenaries, not slaves or so-called savages; initial favorable impressions of blacks were explained and amplified, generation after generation, by poets, historians, and philosophers; the central societies developed a positive image of peripheral Nubia as an independent state of considerable military, political, and cultural importance; both blacks and whites were slaves, but blacks and slaves were never synonymous; black emigrés were not excluded from opportunities available to others of alien extraction, nor were they handicapped in fundamental social relations—they were physically and culturally assimilated; in science, philosophy, and religion, color was not the basis of a widely accepted theory concerning the inferiority of blacks. Reports of imaginary creatures or "uncivilized" tribes inhabiting the extreme south, the somatic norm image of "Mediterranean white," and standard black-white symbolism— all contained the potentiality for the vastly different roles that these factors obviously played in the later development of anti-black sentiments.[247] But the Egyptians, Greeks, Romans, and early Christians were free of what Keith Irvine has described as the "curse of acute color-consciousness, attended by all the raw passion and social problems that cluster around it."[248]

It is difficult to say with certainty what conditions may have been the most influential elements in the formation of the attitude of the ancient world toward blacks.[249] Scholars disagree as to the precise stage in the history of race relations at which color acquired the importance it has assumed in the modern world. One point, however, is certain: the onus of intense color prejudice cannot be placed upon the shoulders of the ancients. The Christian vision[250] of a world in which "there is no question of Greek and Jew, circumcised and uncircumcised, barbarian, Scythian, slave, freeman," owes not a little to earlier views of man in which color played no significant role.

ILLUSTRATIONS

1–2. Reserve heads of an Egyptian prince and his Negroid princess, limestone, from Giza, ca. 2600 B.C.

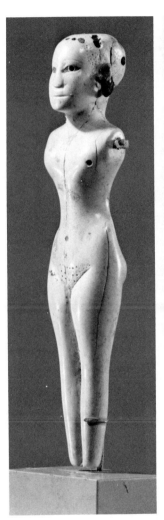

4. Head of a Negro captive, limestone, from Saqqara, ca. 2400–2200 B.C.

3. "Doll," ivory figurine, wearing bronze earrings, provenance unknown, Twelfth Dynasty (ca. 1991–1786 B.C.).

5a–b. Wooden models of forty Nubian archers and detail, from Assiut,
ca. 2000 B.C.

6. Head of a bound Kushite prisoner (detail), limestone,
ca. 1560–1314. B.C.

7a–b. Fragment of a mural painting with blacks bearing tribute of gold and other Nubian products, from tomb of Sebekhotep, Thebes, ca. 1400 B.C.

8a–b. Mural painting and detail of black captives, women, and children, from tomb of Huy, Thebes, ca. 1342–1333 B.C.

10. Head of Taharqa, black basalt, ca. 690–664 B.C.

9. Head of Shabaka from a colossal statue, pink granite, from Karnak, ca. 716–701 B.C.

11. Sphinx of Taharqa, granite, from Kawa, ca. 690–664 B.C.

12. Lion cub attacking a black man, carved ivory plaquette, from Nimrud, seventh century B.C.

13. Ethiopian prisoners captured during Assyrian siege of an Egyptian city, detail of bas-relief, from palace of Ashurbanipal at Nineveh, ca. 669–662 B.C.

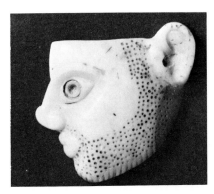

14. Negro profile in shell, from Ayios Onouphrios, Crete, early second millennium B.C.

15. Janiform perfume vase with heads of a black and a bearded white man, faience, from Cyprus, first half of sixth century B.C.

16. Head-vase in the shape of a Negro's head, with tightly coiled hair indicated by raised dots, terracotta, second half of sixth century B.C.

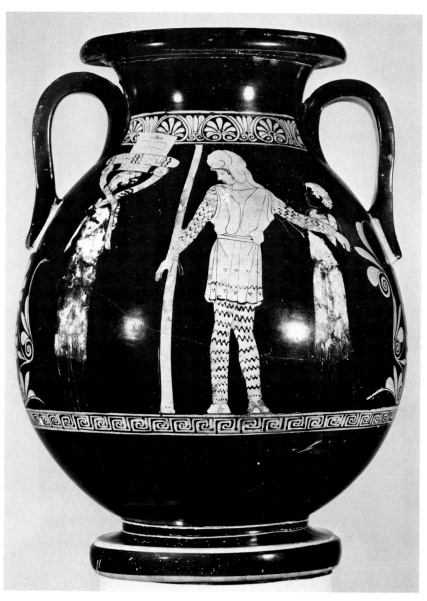

17. Pelike, with detail of Andromeda and woolly-haired black attendant, terracotta, workshop of the Niobid Painter, fifth century B.C.

18. Casts of scarabs, with heads of blacks marked with cicatrices, from Naukratis, sixth century B.C.

19. Pelike, with scene of Heracles and circumcised Negroes, terracotta, Pan Painter, fifth century B.C.

20. Detail of cup, with Heracles and mulatto attendants of Busiris, terracotta, from Vulci, ca. 450 B.C.

21. Detail of a scene from an *Andromeda* on a calyx-krater showing Ethiopia personified as a mulatto, terracotta, from Capua, late fifth century B.C.

22a–b. Head with pronounced Negroid features, terracotta, late third century B.C.

23. Miniature head-vase of an adolescent with less pronounced Negroid features, bronze, ca. 300–100 B.C.

24. Bust of a young Negro prisoner (?), bronze, from Samannûd, second or
first century B.C.

25a–b. Head of a young mulatto girl, marble, from
Corinth, second century A.D.

26. Mosaic of five animal fighters, one a Negro, celebrating at a drinking bout, marble, from Thysdrus (El Djem), first half of third century
A.D.

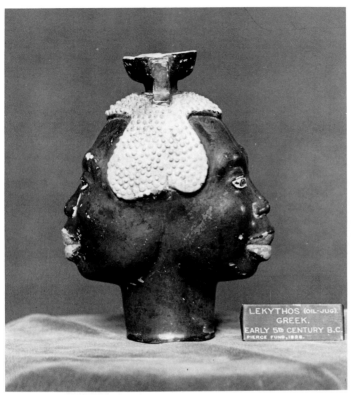

27a–b. Janiform vase in the shape of Negroid heads from the same mold, terracotta, early fifth century B.C., and a Shilluk from the Sudan. Examples of the pronounced Negroid or "pure" type, ancient and modern.

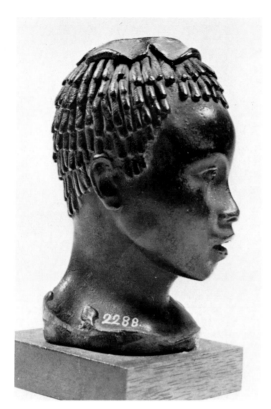

28a–b. Miniature head-vase of a black youth, bronze, third or second century B.C., and a Somali from east Africa. Examples of blacks with less pronounced Negroid features, ancient and modern.

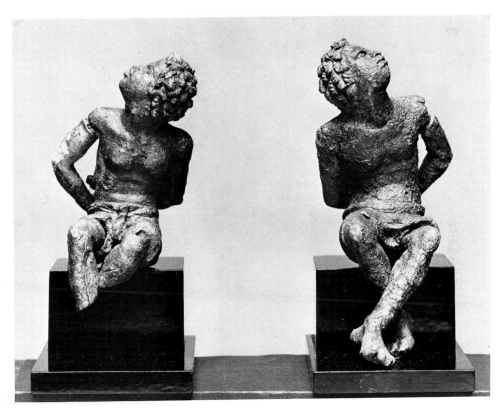

29a–b. Bronze statuettes of Negro captives with arms tied behind the back, late first century B.C.

30. Knob or handle in shape of
three conjoined heads, perhaps a
Meroïtic queen, her consort, and
son, agate, from Egypt, between
second half of first century B.C.
and first century A.D.

31a–b. Obverse of an Etruscan coin, with
head of a Negro mahout, and reverse
with elephant, bronze, third century B.C.

32a,b,c. Herms with heads of a Negro (front and profile) and a Libyan,
black limestone, from Baths of Antoninus Pius, Carthage, mid-second
century A.D.

33. Fragment of a sarcophagus with scene of captives in presence of a Roman general flanked by his soldiers, one a Negro, marble, first half of third century A.D.

34. Protome of a lion's head holding a Negro in its jaws, Egyptian blue, the reign of Amenophis III (1417–1379 B.C.), from Qantir (in the eastern Delta).

35. Footstool, with decoration of chained Kushite and Asiatic captives, wood with overlay of blue glass and gilt stucco, from tomb of Tutankhamun at Thebes, ca. 1342–1333 B.C.

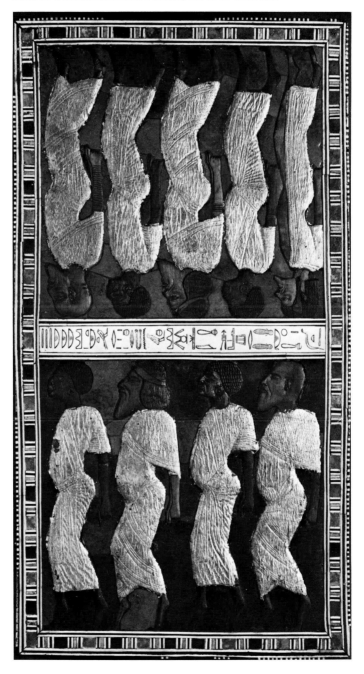

36. Tiles with design of black and white captives, polychrome faience,
from palace of Ramesses III at Medinet Habu, ca. 1198–1166 B.C.

37. Fragment of a relief showing wounded Nubian archer supported by a comrade, sandstone, from Sesebi, late Eighteenth or early Nineteenth Dynasty.

38. Head of Queen Tiy, wife of Amenophis III, wood, from Medinet Ghurab(?), ca. 1385–1362 B.C.

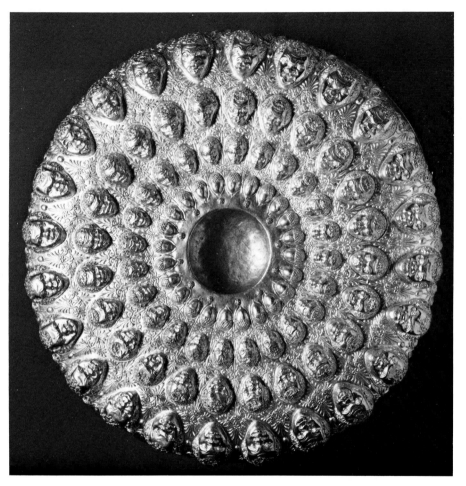

39a–b. Phiale with three concentric rows of Negroid heads and one of acorns, gold, from Panagjurishte, late fourth century B.C.

40a–b. Triobol with helmeted goddess on obverse,
Negro head on reverse, silver,
from Athens, ca. 502 B.C.

41. Statuettes of warriors with double-edged ax and shield, terracotta, from Egypt, Roman period.

42. Detail of an oinochoe depicting a Negroid Nike driving Heracles' chariot, terracotta, from Cyrenaica, fourth century B.C.

43. Detail of skyphos showing a Negroid Circe offering a cup to Odysseus, terracotta, from Kabeirion, late fifth or early fourth century B.C.

44. A Negroid Spinario, terracotta, from Priene, first century B.C.

46. Attic alabastron showing Negro warrior in black outline on a white ground, terracotta, early fifth century B.C.

45. Askos in the shape of a boy sleeping beside an amphora, terracotta, from Taranto, third century B.C.

47. Incense shovel decorated with the head of a Negro boy blowing over the surface of the pan, bronze, third century B.C.

48a,b,c. Statuette of a youthful musician, bronze, Hellenistic,
from Chalon-sur-Saône.

49. Funerary portrait of a
man of mixed black-white
descent, Pentelic marble,
probably from Rome, late
first century B.C. to mid-first
century A.D.

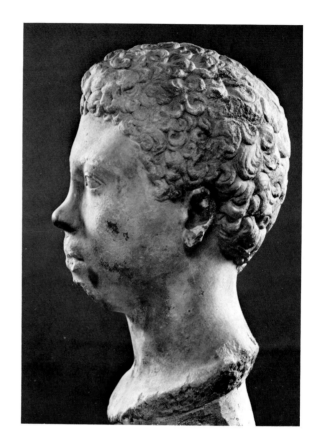

50a–b. Head of a Negro youth, slightly under life-sized, gray marble, from southern Asia Minor (?), second century B.C.

51. Detail from mosaic depicting a black man following a camel, from
El Djem, House of Silenus, late second or early third century A.D.

52. Detail from mosaic of a rural scene showing a Negro fowler placing snares in a tree, from Uthina (Oudna), House of the Laberii, third century A.D.

53. Mosaic depicting servants bringing accessories for a banquet, with a Negroid central figure, from Carthage, third century A.D.

54. Mosaic of wrestlers, one black, from Thaenae, third century A.D.

55. Mosaic of chariot race and black grooms, from Capsa, sixth or
seventh century A.D.

56. Mosaic of a racially mixed couple, C. Julius Serenus and Numitoria
Saturnina, from Thaenae, third or fourth century A.D.

57. Fragment of a sarcophagus, with elderly Negroid "philosopher" in low relief, marble, third century A.D.

58. Head of Juba II, king of Mauretania, marble, from Cherchell, late first century B.C. or early first century A.D.

59. Detail from pelike showing a mulatto Cepheus, terracotta, workshop of the
Niobid Painter, fifth century B.C.

60. Mural painting of black and white priests in an Isiac ceremony,
from Herculaneum, first century A.D.

61. Mural painting of Isiac ritual with black and white cultists and a ceremonial dance performed by a Negro, from Herculaneum, first century A.D.

62. Ampulla, with profile of Negroid St. Menas,
terracotta, fifth to seventh century A.D.

Notes and Sources

Sources of Illustrations

Index

Abbreviations

ANET   *Ancient Near Eastern Texts Relating to the Old Testament*

ARE   *Ancient Records of Egypt: Historical Documents*

CAH   *Cambridge Ancient History*

CCL   *Corpus Christianorum, Series Latina*

GCS   *Die griechischen christlichen Schriftsteller der ersten drei Jahrhunderte*

GGM   *Geographi Graeci Minores*

PG   *Patrologiae Cursus Completus, Series Graeca*

PL   *Patrologiae Cursus Completus, Series Latina*

RBA   *Review of Snowden, Blacks in Antiquity*

NOTES AND SOURCES

1. Who Were the African Blacks?

1. The basic sources of the black-white relations examined in this study are Egyptian, Greek, Roman, and early Christian. Important supplementary material, however, appears in the Old Testament and Assyrian documents. Both of these sources provide pertinent information concerning the Kushites during the Egyptian and Napatan periods; the Kushites of the Old Testament figure prominently in the early Christian image of blacks.

2. For examples of the terminology used for Nubia and Nubians in recent studies, see the following: B. G. Trigger, *Nubia under the Pharaohs* (London 1976); J. Vercoutter, J. Leclant, F. M. Snowden, Jr., and J. Desanges, *The Image of the Black in Western Art, I: From the Pharaohs to the Fall of the Roman Empire* [hereafter cited *Image of the Black*] (New York 1976); W. Y. Adams, *Nubia: Corridor to Africa* (London 1977); S. Hochfield and E. Riefstahl, eds., *Africa in Antiquity: The Arts of Ancient Nubia and the Sudan, I: The Essays* [hereafter *Africa in Antiquity*] (Brooklyn 1978); S. Wenig, *Africa in Antiquity, II: The Catalogue* (Brooklyn 1978); D. Neiman, "Ethiopia and Kush: Biblical and Ancient Geography," *The Ancient World* 3 (1980) 35–42.

3. See K. H. Priese, "The Napatan Period," pp. 75–88, and F. Hintze, "The Meroitic Period," pp. 89–105, in *Africa in Antiquity*.

4. See Strabo 17.3.24 on the difficulties of determining the boundaries of Ethiopia and Libya; cf. Pliny *Naturalis historia* 5.4.30.

5. See Desanges, "The Iconography of the Black in Ancient North Africa," in *Image of the Black*, pp. 246–250.

6. Vercoutter, "The Iconography of the Black in Ancient Egypt: From the Beginnings to the Twenty-fifth Dynasty," in *Image of the Black*, figs. 3–7.

7. The "Hymn to the Aten" in its anthropological differentiations of the races of mankind makes only one reference to skin color: "their skins are different." W. K. Simpson, ed., *The Literature of Ancient Egypt: An Anthology of Stories, Instructions and Poetry* (New Haven 1972), p. 293. An inscription from the reign of Tuthmosis I describing an Egyptian victory in Nubia boasts that "there is not a remnant among the Curly-Haired." J. H.

Breasted, *Ancient Records of Egypt: Historical Documents,* II: *The Eighteenth Dynasty* [hereafter *ARE*], reissue (New York 1962) p. 30. For Greek and Roman descriptions, see F. M. Snowden, Jr., *Blacks in Antiquity: Ethiopians in the Greco-Roman Experience [hereafter Blacks in Antiquity]* (Cambridge 1970) pp. 1–12.

8. See Vercoutter, *Image of the Black,* p. 34.

9. Ibid., for Nubian archers (figs. 10–11) from Assiut and a Negro mercenary from Gebelein (fig. 12) and p. 43; see also fig. 5 above.

10. Jeremiah 13:23 (Revised Standard Version). *The New English Bible with the Apocrypha* (Oxford and Cambridge 1970) uses "Nubian" instead of "Ethiopian." For Ebed-melech's rescue of the prophet, see Jeremiah 38:7–14.

11. Lucian *Adversus indoctum* 28; cf. Palatine Anthology 11:428; *Corpus Paroemiographorum Graecorum,* I, Zenobius 1.46 (p. 18) and Diogenianus 1.45 (p. 187); II, Diogenianus 1.19 (p. 4) and Apostolius 1.68 (p. 258).

12. Ibn Khaldûn, *The Muqaddimah: An Introduction to History* (Bollingen Series XLIII), trans. F. Rosenthal (New York 1958) I, 172.

13. For the effect of the sun on the Ethiopian's skin color, see Herodotus 2.22; Aristotle *Problemata* 10.66.898b; Lucretius 6.722, 1109; Vitruvius *De architectura* 6.1.3-4; Manilius *Astronomica* 4.758–759; Ovid *Metamorphoses* 2.235–236; Pliny *Naturalis historia* 2.80.189; Lucan 10.221–222; Seneca *Quaestiones naturales* 4A.2.18; Ptolemy *Tetrabiblos* 2.2.56.

14. Manilius 4.722–730.

15. Arrian *Anabasis* 5.4.4; Pliny *Naturalis historia* 6.22.70; Arrian *Indica* 6.6.9.

16. Boethius *In Porphyrium commentaria* 5 (*PL* 64.157) mentions degrees of blackness varying from what borders on dark (*fuscis proxima*) to very black (*nigerrima*). *Fuscus* (dark) usually indicated a lighter hue than *niger* (cf. Sidonius *Epistulae* 2.10.4—if a man of dark skin (*fuscus*) dresses in white, he becomes blacker (*nigrior*). Martial (7.13) says that dark (*fusca*) Lycoris, after a visit to Tibur, where she thought the sun had a bleaching effect, returned black (*nigra*).

17. Agatharchides *De Mari Erythraeo* 58 *Geographi Graeci Minores* [hereafter *GGM*] I, 148; Diodorus 3.29.1.

18. Ptolemy *Geographia* 1.9.7 (edition, C. Müller, vol. 1, pt. 1 [Paris 1883], pt. 2 [Paris 1901]; pt. 1, p. 25).

19. Flavius Philostratus *Vita Apollonii* 6.2.

20. Trigger, "Nubian, Negro, Black, Nilotic?" in *Africa in Antiquity,* p. 27.

21. For the most detailed studies of the nomenclature and description of Ethiopian peoples in northwest Africa, see J. Desanges, *Catalogue des tribus africaines de l'antiquité classique à l'ouest du Nil,* Publications de la

Section Histoire, no. 4 (Dakar 1962), and *Recherches sur l'activité des méditerranéens aux confins de l'Afrique (VIe siècle avant J.C.–IVe siècle après J.C.)—Collection de l'Ecole Française de Rome*, 38 [hereafter *Recherches*] (Rome 1978).

22. Pliny *Naturalis historia* 5.8.43 locates the Nigritae among the Ethiopians, but they are not so designated by all the sources: cf. Desanges, *Catalogue*, pp. 226–227, and *Image of the Black*, p. 247; Ptolemy *Geographia* 4.6.5 (Müller pt. 2, pp. 642, 743).

23. Frontinus *Strategemata* 1.11.18.

24. *Anthologia Latina*, ed. A. Riese and F. Bücheler (Leipzig 1894) I, no. 183, pp. 155–156, and no. 353, p. 277; M. Rosenblum, *Luxorius: A Latin Poet among the Vandals*, Records of Civilization Sources and Studies, 62 (New York and London 1961) 150–151; Corippus 6.92–94, *Flavii Cresconii Iohannidos seu de Bellis Libycis VIII*, J. Diggle and F. R. D. Goodyear (Cambridge, Eng. 1970); cf. S. Gsell, *Histoire ancienne de l'Afrique du Nord*, 3rd rev. ed. (Paris 1928) I, 298.

25. Fulgentius *Epistulae* 11–12 (PL 65.378–392).

26. Ptolemy *Geographia* 4.6.5–6 (Müller, pt. 2, pp. 743–745); Desanges, *Catalogue*, pp. 219–220, and *Recherches*, p. 140; Orosius *Adversum paganos* 1.2.88, *Corpus Scriptorum Ecclesiasticorum Latinorum* [hereafter CSEL] V, 32.

27. Diodorus 20.57.5; Desanges, *Catalogue*, p. 80.

28. Solinus 30.2; Isidore *Origines* 9.2.128; Desanges, *Catalogue*, pp. 93–96; *Image of the Black*, p. 247. Strabo 2.5.33; 17.3.19.

29. Lucan 4.679; Arnobius *Adversus nationes* 6.5; Ptolemy *Geographia* 1.9.7 (pt. 1, p. 25).

30. Ptolemy *Geographia* 1.8.5 (pt. 1, pp. 21–22); 4.6.5 (pt. 2, pp. 742–743).

31. Mosaic of the Gladiators, from Zliten, House of Dar Buc Ammera, Tripoli, Archaeological Museum, *Image of the Black*, figs. 339, 368, and p. 247. See Chapter Two, note 69, for Moorish cavalry with corkscrew curls on Trajan's column.

32. *Niger*, Silius Italicus 2.439; Juvenal 5.53–54; *adustus*, Silius Italicus 8.267. Other comments and comparisons with Indians and Ethiopians on the skin color of the Mauri are worthy of note. Isidore *Origines* 14.5.10 states that Mauretania gets its name from the color of its people, for the Greeks render *nigrum* as *mauron*. Manilius 4.729–730 also notes that the Mauri derive their name from the color of their skin. Lucan 4.678–679 says that the Moors are as black as Indians (*concolor Indo Maurus*), who, according to Sidonius *Carmina* 11.106–107, have the same color as Ethiopians (*concolor Aethiopi ... Indus*). Herodotus (3.101) had mentioned some Indians who resembled Ethiopians in color. Arrian *Anabasis* 5.5.4 states that

the Indians Alexander visited were said to be blacker than the rest of mankind, with the exception of the Ethiopians; and Pliny *Historia naturalis* 6.22.70 writes that the Indians south of the Ganges were browned by the sun but not so much as Ethiopians; they became darker as they approached the Indus River.

33. Desanges, *Image of the Black*, p. 268. L. Bertholon and E. Chantre in a study of black-white crossings in ancient and modern northwest Africa, *Recherches anthropologiques dans la Berbérie orientale, Tripolitaine, Tunisie, Algérie*, I (Lyon 1913), comment on the degrees of Negro admixture as evidenced by the extent to which Negroid physical characteristics appear in north African peoples. R. Bartoccini, "Quali erano i caraterri somatici degli antichi Libi?" *Aegyptus* 3 (1922) 165–166, calls attention to racial crossings between Libyans and Negroes from the interior by noting the Negroid (broad) nose and curly or woolly hair of figures in mosaics from Tripolitania whom he considers black-white crosses. O. Bates, *The Eastern Libyans* (London 1914) pp. 43–45, in his study of Negroid Libyans includes the criteria of platyrrhiny and thick lips. Martial's phrase, a Moor with tightly coiled hair—*retorto crine Maurus* (6.39.6) suggests a Negroid type.

34. Xenophanes, Frg. 16 (Diels); Herodotus 7.70.

35. Diodorus 3.8.2.

36. Petronius *Satyricon* 102.

37. *Moretum* 31–35. Another detailed description of blacks has been attributed to classical antiquity by the Arab historian Mas'ūdī (died ca. 956): "Galen mentions ten specific characteristics of blacks—frizzly hair, thin eyebrows, broad nostrils, thick lips, pointed teeth, smelly skin, black pupils, furrowed feet and hands, developed genitalia, and excessive merriment. This author explains this last quality in the black as a result of the imperfect organization of his brain, whence also derives the weakness of his intellect." See Mas'ūdī, *Les Prairies d'or*, trans. C. Barbier de Meynard and J. B. Pavet de Courteille, rev. C. Pellat (Paris 1962) I, 69. Mas'ūdī does not specify the name of the work by Galen in which he or his source found the description; nor does this or any similar passage, as far as I have been able to determine, appear in any extant work of Galen or any other author from the Greco-Roman period. C. Brockelmann in *The Encylopaedia of Islam: A Dictionary of the Geography, Ethnography and Biography of the Muhammadan Peoples*, ed. M. T. Houtsma, et al., III (Leiden and London 1936) 403, s.v. Al-Mas'ūdī, states that the Arab historian and geographer never went into original sources but made superficial inquiries and accepted legends and tales uncritically. Only two of the physical features of blacks attributed to Galen by Mas'ūdī—black color (*De elementis ex Hippocrate* 1.6 [all Galen references from C. G. Kühn's edition], I, 461; *De temperamentis* 2.6, I, 628)

and woolly or frizzly hair (De temperamentis 2.5, I, 616; De usu partium corporis humani 11.14, III, 909–910) appear in Galen. The other characteristics mentioned by Mas'ūdī resemble those found in Arab and Muslim writers rather than in classical sources, which describe most frequently the Ethiopian's color, hair, nose, and lips. For descriptions of blacks in some Arab and Muslim writers from the eighth to the eleventh centuries which resemble Mas'ūdī's catalogue, see B. Lewis, Race and Color in Islam (New York 1971), pp. 17, 33–36.

38. Herodotus 3.20 states that the Ethiopians against whom Cambyses sent troops were the tallest men in the world; Pliny Naturalis historia 7.2.31 cites Crates of Pergamum as his source for the report that the Ethiopian Syrbotae were more than eight cubits (some twelve feet, obviously an exaggeration) in height; and Scylax Periplus 112 GGM I, 94, writes that a group of western Ethiopians were the tallest race of men, with heights of more than four cubits.

39. For circumcision among Ethiopians, see Herodotus 2.104, Diodorus 3.32.4, Josephus Contra Apionem 1.169, and the circumcised Negroes in a Busiris scene on a fifth-century B.C. pelike by the Pan Painter in Athens (no. 9683), Snowden, Blacks in Antiquity, fig. 4 and p. 23.

40. For facial cicatrices in Ethiopians, see Petronius Satyricon 102, and for examples in sixth-century B.C. molds from Naukratis, see Snowden, Image of the Black, fig. 148 and p. 140. For scarification in the form of three parallel scars on each cheek, from the Roman period, see Snowden, Image of the Black, fig. 319. For earlier examples from Nubia, see Lecant, "Kushites and Meroites: Iconography of the African Rulers in the Ancient Upper Nile," Image of the Black, pp. 128, 297, and figs. 139–140, and for persistence of the practice in the present-day Sudan, see Adams, Nubia, p. 46.

41. Philostratus Vita Apollonii 3.11. and Vitae Sophistarum 2.558. The mention of a shining crescent-shaped spot that appeared on the face of Memnon, the Ethiopian pupil of Herodes Atticus, as a youth but disappeared later may be an early reference to vitiligo, a skin abnormality, particularly noticeable in blacks, characterized by loss of pigment in areas of different sizes and shapes. Cf. P. Graindor, Un Milliardaire antique: Hérode Atticus et sa famille (Cairo 1930) pp. 114–116 (Université Egyptienne, Recueil de travaux publiés par la faculté des lettres, fasc. 5); Image of the Black, figs. 336–338.

42. See also Vercoutter, Image of the Black, pp. 38, 41, and fig. 7. C. Aldred, Old Kingdom Art in Ancient Egypt (London 1949) p. 30, points out that it is difficult to deny, as some have, that the princess has Negroid characteristics, and adds that somewhat "alien un-Egyptian" features appear in the royal family of this period.

43. Vercoutter, *Image of the Black*, p. 41 and fig. 8. The figures reproduced in this book are often included in *Image of the Black* in different views, in color, or with fuller textual discussion.

44. Ibid., figs. 3, 5–6 and pp. 36, 38.

45. Leiden, Rijksmuseum van Oudheden, F. 1947/9.1; and H. G. Fischer, "The Nubian Mercenaries of Gebelein during the First Intermediate Period," *Kush* 9 (1961) 56–80.

46. Vercoutter, *Image of the Black*, p. 43 and figs. 10–11.

47. For mural paintings of Kushite men, women, and children from Theban tombs, see ibid., figs. 14–16 (tomb of Rekhmire, ca. 1504–1450 B.C.), fig. 19 (tomb of Inene, ca. 1557–1504 B.C.); fig. 20 (tomb of Horemheb, ca. 1425–1408 B.C.).

48. Ibid., p. 62, and figs. 17–18, 24–26.

49. Leclant, ibid., p. 90 and fig. 67.

50. Ibid., pp. 96, 98, 104, and figs. 81–92; Wenig, *Africa in Antiquity* II, 48–53, and figs. 24, 26, 27; J. M. Plumley, "Qaṣr Ibrîm," *Journal of Egyptian Archaeology* 61 (1975) 19–20.

51. Leclant, *Image of the Black*, p. 116.

52. A. Parrot, *Assur* (Paris 1961) pp. 152–153 and figs. 186–187; Leclant, *Image of the Black*, p. 109 and fig. 96.

53. For one of the stelae found at Zenjirli, see D. D. Luckenbill, *Ancient Records of Assyria and Babylonia*, II: *Historical Records of Assyria from Sargon to the End* (Chicago 1927) pp. 224–227, and Parrot, *Assur*, p. 34, fig. 39C, and p. 366; for the other stele erected at Til Barsib in northern Syria, Parrot, *Assur* p. 77, fig. 86, and p. 368.

54. J. B. Pritchard, ed., *Ancient Near Eastern Texts Relating to the Old Testament* [hereafter *ANET*] 3rd ed. (Princeton 1969) p. 293; S. Smith, chap. 3 (Sennacherib and Esarhaddon) in *Cambridge Ancient History* III (1970) 85–86; Leclant, *Image of the Black*, p. 109.

55. R. D. Barnett, *Assyrian Sculpture in the British Museum* (London 1975) plate 177.

56. W. S. Smith, *Interconnections in the Ancient Near East: A Study of the Relationships between the Arts of Egypt, the Aegean, and Western Asia* (New Haven 1965) p. 56.

57. Snowden, *Image of the Black*, fig. 142 and p. 136.

58. Herakleion, Archeological Museum; A. Evans, *The Palace of Minos at Knossos* II, pt. 2 (London 1928) 755–757 and plate 13; Snowden, ibid., p. 136 and fig. 145.

59. Athens, National Museum; Snowden, ibid., p. 138 and fig. 147. S. Marinatos, *Excavations at Thera V, 1971 Season* (Athens 1972) p. 43, plates 100–101, and color plate J, calls attention to the exceedingly thick lips of a

priestess (with a big ring or disk hanging from one ear) and raises the question whether the thick lips (which he noted also in the African profile) were characteristic of certain families.

60. Chora, Archaeological Museum; Snowden, ibid., p. 138, fig. 146, and M. L. Lang, *The Palace of Nestor at Pylos in Western Messenia*, II: *The Frescoes* (Princeton 1969) pp. 61–62, 94, and plates 44, 129, 129D.

61. For the geographical areas of the blacks of classical artists, see the maps in this book; for Negroid types in Greek and Roman art, see illustrations in *Image of the Black*, pp. 133–245, 247–268.

62. Ibid., pp. 139–140; figs. 159–160 and p. 146.

63. Ibid., figs. 153–154 and pp. 140, 144.

64. Ibid., figs. 174–175 and p. 155.

65. Ibid., fig. 148 and pp. 139–140.

66. Herodotus 2.104.

67. *Image of the Black*, figs. 171–172 and p. 152.

68. Ibid., pp. 155, 160.

69. Ibid., fig. 197 and p. 166. For a servant girl with similar mulatto features and her mistress at a child's tomb, see the white-ground lekythos, ca. 460–450 B.C., attributed to the Thanatos Painter, H. A. Shapiro, *Art, Myth, and Culture: Greek Vases from Southern Collections* (New Orleans 1981) pp. 112–113, fig. 44.

70. Aristotle *De generatione animalium* 1.18.722a; *Historia animalium* 7.6.585b. For contacts of Elis with Egypt during the Twenty-sixth Dynasty, see W. Decker, "La délégation des Eléens en Egypte sous la 26e dynastie (Hér. II 160–Diod. I 95)," *Chronique d'Egypte* 49 (1974) 31–42. For other examples of interest in black-white racial mixture, see Pliny *Naturalis historia* 7.12.51 and Plutarch *De sera numinis vindicta* 21 (563).

71. Snowden, *Image of the Black*, pp. 188–190.

72. Ibid., fig. 239 and p. 188.

73. J. L. Angel, review of Snowden, *Blacks in Antiquity*, in *American Anthropologist* 74 (1972) 159.

74. See figs. 60–61 below; and Snowden, *Image of the Black*, figs. 288–289 and pp. 221–222.

75. J. W. Salomonson, *Mosaïques romaines de Tunisie: Catalogue* (Brussels 1964) pp. 33–34 and plate 19; Chapter Four below, notes 66, 69–70.

76. Desanges, *Image of the Black*, p. 247.

77. Trigger, "Nubian, Negro, Black, Nilotic?" in *Africa in Antiquity*, p. 27.

78. Adams, *Nubia*, p. 8.

79. J. Russell, review of *The Image of the Black in Western Art*, vols. 1 and 2, in *New York Times Book Review*, June 29, 1980, p. 24.

80. E. A. Hooton, *Up from the Ape,* rev. ed. (New York 1946) pp. 619–620, 662, in listing the outstanding features of the specialized Negroid division of mankind; and M. J. Herskovits, *Encyclopaedia Britannica* (Chicago, London, Toronto 1960) s.v. "Negro," XVI, 193, in a description of Negroid traits in their most marked form, the so-called true Negro.

81. M. J. Herskovits, *The American Negro: A Study in Racial Crossing* (Bloomington 1964) pp. 19–20.

82. See C. B. Day, *A Study of Some Negro-White Families in the United States,* with foreword by E. A. Hooton (Cambridge, Mass. 1932). For examples of mixed types, see plates 1c, 1d, 4b, 5, 13, 15, 16, 35, 50.

2. Meetings of Blacks and Whites

1. *Cambridge Ancient History* [hereafter *CAH*], 3rd ed., I, pt. 2, pp. 50–51; Leclant, "Egypt in Nubia during the Old, Middle, and New Kingdoms," in *Africa in Antiquity,* p. 63.

2. Breasted, *ARE* I, 65–66, sec. 146.

3. *ARE* I, 163, sec. 358–359.

4. See above, Chapter One, note 44.

5. *CAH* I, pt. 2, pp. 360–361; and *ARE* I, 142–143, sec. 311–312.

6. M. Lichtheim, *Ancient Egyptian Literature: A Book of Readings, I: The Old and Middle Kingdoms* (Berkeley 1975) p. 90; and H. G. Fischer, "The Nubian Mercenaries," *Kush* 9 (1961) 44–56 and plate 10.

7. *CAH* I, pt. 2, pp. 506–507; Adams, *Nubia* pp. 176–182 and plates 6, 7a. Adams (pp. 183–188) argues that the forts were constructed not merely for military protection against hostile Nubians but also for the economic purpose of keeping the Nile under Egyptian control.

8. *CAH* I, pt. 2, p. 508; cf. Leclant, *Africa in Antiquity* p. 63.

9. *ARE,* I, 293, para. 652.

10. *CAH* II, pt. 1, 3rd ed., pp. 296–298; *ANET,* p. 232.

11. *ANET,* p. 555.

12. Figs. 8a–8b above; in color, Vercoutter, *Image of the Black,* figs. 24–26.

13. *ARE* II, 30, sec. 71.

14. Vercoutter, *Image of the Black,* p. 46.

15. For recent summaries of the Napatan and Meroïtic kingdoms of Kush, see K. H. Priese, "The Kingdom of Kush: The Napatan Period," and F. Hintze, "The Kingdom of Kush: The Meroitic Period," in *Africa in Antiquity,* pp. 75–105.

16. *CAH* II, pt. 2, pp. 631–634; cf. D. O'Connor, "Ancient Egypt and Black Africa—Early Contacts," *Expedition: The Magazine of Archaeol-*

ogy/Anthropology 14 (1971) 9; cf. H. Frankfort, *The Birth of Civilization in the Near East* (Bloomington, 1951) p. 90.

17. 2 Chronicles 14:9; Josephus *Antiquitates* 8:292; K. A. Kitchen, *The Third Intermediate Period in Egypt, 1100-650 B.C.* (Warminster 1973), p. 309.

18. For details of the Twenty-fifth Dynasty, see Kitchen, chaps. 10, 23.

19. *ARE* IV, 419-444.

20. *ANET*, p. 293; Luckenbill, *Ancient Records of Assyria and Babylonia*, and Parrot, *Assur*.

21. The carefully documented study of Desanges, *Recherches sur l'activité des méditerranéens aux confins de l' Afrique*, is an invaluable source of information on important aspects of contacts between Mediterranean whites and Ethiopians for the period from the sixth century B.C. to the fourth century A.D.

22. Kitchen, *Third Intermediate Period*, p. 406.

23. S. Sauneron and J. Yoyotte, "La Campagne nubienne de Psammétique II et sa signification historique," *Bulletin de l'Institut français d'archéologie orientale du Caire* 50 (1952) 157-207.

24. M. N. Tod, *A Selection of Greek Historical Inscriptions*, 2nd ed. (Oxford 1946) no. 4, pp. 6-7, and A. Bernand and O. Masson, "Les Inscriptions grecques d'Abou-Simbel," *Revue des études grecques* 70 (1957) 3-20, Xenophanes Frg. 16 (Diels).

25. Snowden, *Image of the Black*, p. 144, figs. 155-158.

26. Herodotus 2.182 states that Amasis was the first conqueror of Cyprus, where stone figures of Negroes (dated not later than 560 B.C.), probably in the employ of Amasis, have been found. The figures from Ayia Irini are described and reproduced in E. Gjerstad, J. Lindros, E. Sjöquist, and A. Westholm, *The Swedish Cyprus Expedition, Finds and Results of the Excavations in Cyprus: 1927-1931*, II (Stockholm 1935) plate 239, nos. 1095 and 1228, and E. Gjerstad, *The Swedish Cyprus Expedition, IV: The Cypro-Geometric Cypro-Archaic and Cypro-Classical Periods* (Stockholm 1948) pp. 103-104, 466-467. See Desanges, *Recherches*, p. 227, for a Nubian campaign of Amasis and his employment of Nubians.

27. Herodotus 2.160 and Diodorus 1.95. Herodotus gives the name of the Egyptian king consulted as Psammis; Diodorus, as Amasis. On this point see W. Decker, "La délégation des Eléens en Egypte sous la 26 dynastie (Hér. II 160—Diod. I, 95)," *Chronique d'Egypte* 49 (1974) 31-42.

28. Aristotle *De generatione animalium* 1.18.722a.

29. Herodotus 2.29.

30. Pliny *Naturalis historia* 6.35.183.

31. Herodotus 7.69-70.

32. Snowden, *Image of the Black*, pp. 148-167.

33. Herodotus 2.137, 139.

34. Adams, *Nubia,* pp. 329, 344–349, 365–374.

35. P. L. Shinnie, Meroe: *A Civilization of the Sudan* (New York 1967) p. 169.

36. P. M. Fraser, *Ptolemaic Alexandria,* I (Oxford 1972) pp. 175–179; see Desanges, *Recherches,* pp. 247–305, 377–379, for Ptolemaic interest in elephants as well as for general Ptolemaic activity in Ethiopia.

37. Diodorus 1.37.5; cf. Desanges, *Recherches,* pp. 252–279.

38. Theocritus, 17.87; Diodorus 3.36.3; Strabo 16.4.7–8, 16.4.10, 16.4.13, 17.1.5; Pliny *Naturalis historia* 6.34.171; Periplus Maris Erythraei 3, *GGM,* II, 258–259; Athenaeus 5.201.

39. A third-century B.C. papyrus that includes the statement that "Ethiopians came down and besieged" and that mentions countermeasures seems to refer to Ethiopian initiative in attacking an unnamed town. See F. Preisigke, *Sammelbuch griechisher Urkunden aus Ägypten* I (Strasbourg 1915) no. 5111, and C. Préaux, "Sur les communications de l'Ethiopie avec l'Egypte hellénistique," *Chronique d'Egypte* 27 (1952) 263–264.

40. C. Préaux, "Esquisse d'une histoire des révolutions égyptiennes sous les Lagides," *Chronique d'Egypte* 11 (1936) 535–536; P. W. Pestman, "Harmachis et Anchmachis, deux rois indigènes du temps des Ptolémées, *Chronique d'Egypte* 40 (1965) 168–169; B. G. Haycock, "Landmarks in Cushite History," *Journal of Egyptian Archaeology* 58 (1972) 234.

41. Agatharchides *De Mari Erythraeo* 20 *GGM,* I, 119, and Fraser, *Ptolemaic Alexandria,* pp. 541–542; Desanges, *Recherches,* pp. 281–282.

42. Shinnie, *Meroe,* p. 101; Hintze, *Civilizations of the Old Sudan,* pp. 23, 25; B. G. Haycock, "Landmarks in Cushite History," *Journal of Egyptian Archaeology* 53 (1972) 230, 237; cf. notes 55 and 57 below.

43. Pliny *Naturalis historia* 6.35.183.

44. Strabo 2.3.5; cf. Fraser, *Ptolemaic Alexandria,* pp. 182–184, and Desanges, *Recherches,* pp. 151–173.

45. For the relations of the Roman Empire with Nilotic Africa for the period from Augusus to Theodosius I, see Desanges, *Recherches,* pp. 307–366. For the ancient sources on Rome and the Ethiopians during the time of Augustus, see Strabo, 17.1.53–54; Pliny *Naturalis historia* 6.35.181–182; Dio Cassius 54.5.4–6; *CIL* III, 14147.5; H. Dessau, *Inscriptiones Latinae Selectae* [hereafter *ILS*] III (Berlin 1916) no. 8995.

46. The bronze statuettes of Negro captives in East Berlin, Staatliche Museen, Antikensammlung, Br. 10485–10486, of the late first century B.C. may be a record of the prisoners taken in the campaigns of Petronius; see K. A. Neugebauer, "Aus der Werkstatt eines griechischen Toreuten in Aegypten," *Schumacher-Festschrift* (Mainz 1930) p. 236 and plate 23.

47. The woman in fig. 30 has been interpreted as a Meroïtic queen by C. T. Seltman, "Two Heads of Negresses," *American Journal of Archaeology* 24 (1920) 18–22.

48. S. Jameson, "Chronology of the Campaign of Aelius Gallus and C. Petronius," *Journal of Roman Studies* 58 (1968) 82.

49. Pliny *Naturalis historia* 6.35.181; Seneca *Quaestiones naturales* 6.8.3. For modern views on Nero's Ethiopian interests, see Anderson in *CAH* X, 778–779; L. P. Kirwan, "Rome beyond the Southern Egyptian Frontier," *Geographical Journal* 123 (1957) 16; Desanges, *Recherches*, pp. 323–325.

50. A. Vogliano, *Un Papiro storico greco della Raccolta Milanese e le campagne dei romani in Etiopia* (Milan 1940) pp. 1–24. Cf. E. G. Turner, "Papyrus 40 'della Raccolta Milanese,' " *Journal of Roman Studies* 40 (1950) 57–59.

51. Shinnie, *Meroe*, p. 49; Snowden, *Blacks in Antiquity*, pp. 134–135.

52. Blemmyes as a black-skinned Ethiopian race (*Scholia in Theocritum Vetera* 7.114a—C. Wendel's edition, p. 106); as burnt-colored (Dionysius "Periegetes" *Orbis descriptio* 220 GGM III, 114); as black-skinned (Avienus *Descriptio orbis terrae* 330 GGM III, 180); as woolly-haired (Nonnus *Dionysiaca* 26.341). Cf. Adams, *Nubia*, pp. 389, 419, and "Geography and Population of the Nile Valley," in *Africa in Antiquity*, pp. 22–23, and fig. 7.

53. Desanges, *Recherches*, pp. 341–366; Snowden, *Blacks in Antiquity*, pp. 136–141.

54. Procopius *De bello Persico* 1.19.29–35.

55. F. Panvini Rosati, "La monetazione annibalica," in *Studi Annibalici, Atti del Convegno svoltosi a Cortona, Tuoro sul Trasimeno, Perugia, Ottobre 1961*, V, n.s. (1961–1964) [Cortona 1964], pp. 178–80; cf. J. Desanges, "Les Chasseurs d'éléphants d'Abou-Simbel," *Actes du quatre-vingt-douzième Congrès National des Sociétés Savantes*, Section d'Archéologie, Strasbourg et Colmar 1967, (Paris 1970) p. 36, note 28; H. H. Scullard, "Hannibal's Elephants," *The Numismatic Chronicle* [hereafter NC] 8, 6th series (1948) 163; W. Gowers and H. H. Scullard, "Hannibal's Elephants Again," *NC* 10 (1950) 279–280; E. S. G. Robinson, "Carthaginian and Other South Italian Coins of the Second Punic War," *NC* 4, 7th series (1964) 47; Snowden, *Image of the Black*, pp. 212–213 and figs. 271–274.

56. Plautus *Poenulus* 1289–1291.

57. Cf. Seneca *Epistulae* 85.41; Martial 1.104, lines 9–10, 6.77.8; Achilles Tatius 4.4.6; Arrian *Tactica* 2.2 and 19.6. See Hintze, "The Meroitic Period," in *Africa in Antiquity*, pp. 89, 93, and fig. 61; *Africa in Antiquity* II, 66, 77, 210, and fig. 38.

58. See Chapter One, notes 28–31.

59. Tacitus *Historiae* 4.50.

60. Pliny *Naturalis historia* 5.5.36; cf Desanges, *Recherches,* pp. 190–195.

61. Tacitus *Annales* 4.23–24, 4.26.

62. Tacitus *Historiae* 4.50.

63. Ptolemy *Geographia* 1.8.4; Desanges, *Recherches,* pp. 197–213, 375, and pp. 198–200 on the problem of the location of Agisymba.

64. See also figs. 358–359 in *Image of the Black.*

65. Ammianus Marcellinus 29.5.37.

66. Corippus, *Johannis,* who describes two of the Mauri as black: 8.415–416 ("nigro de corpore sanguis emicat") and 8.482 ("nigri ... Mamonis").

67. Scriptores Historiae Augustae, *Septimius Severus* 22.4–5; R. G. Collingwood and R. P. Wright, *The Roman Inscriptions of Britain* (Oxford 1965) I, 626, no. 2042; cf. A. Birley, *Septimius Severus: The African Emperor* (London 1971), pp. 265–266.

68. L. Salerno, *Palazzo Rondinini* (Rome 1965) p. 259, no. 85 and fig. 139; *Image of the Black,* fig. 281 and p. 214; Snowden, *Blacks in Antiquity,* pp. 142, 228, and fig. 86; R. Brilliant *The Arch of Septimius Severus in the Roman Forum,* Memoirs of the American Academy in Rome, vol. 29 (Rome 1967) plates 78c,d, 80a, 81, and p. 247.

69. See L. Rossi, *Trajan's Column and the Dacian Wars,* trans. J. M. C. Toynbee (London 1971), for comment on the corkscrew curls of the Moorish cavalry on Trajan's column, pp. 104, 162, and fig. 54 on p. 163; cf. M. P. Speidel, "The Rise of the Ethnic Units in the Roman Imperial Army," pp. 202–231 in H. Temporini, ed. *Aufstieg und Niedergang der römischen Welt* II.3 (Berlin and New York 1975) and plate 1 with a caption that calls attention to the "characteristically braided hair" of the Moorish horsemen. E. A. Hooton, *Up from the Ape,* rev. ed. (New York 1946) p. 483, points out that kinky or frizzly hair ordinarily appears in racial types in which there is at least a generous admixture of Negro or Negrito; cf. J. H. Lewis, *The Biology of the Negro* (Chicago 1941) p. 61. In view of modern anthropological observations on the hair of mixed black-white types, the representation of the Moorish cavalry on Trajan's column is worthy of note and, like classical notices on the color of the Garamantes and the Mauri (Chapter One above, notes 29–33), may point to the accuracy of ancient artists in depicting racially mixed types in northwest Africa.

70. For the view that Lusius Quietus was Negroid or Ethiopian, see the series of articles by W. den Boer in *Mnemosyne* 1 (1948) 327–337; 3 (1950) 263–267, 339–343. A. G. Ross questions den Boer's arguments in *Mnemosyne*

3 (1950) 158–164, 336–338, as does L. Petersen, "Lusius Quietus," *Das Altertum* 14 (1968) 212. Desanges, *Image of the Black,* p. 312, n. 148, suggests that the commander of the Moorish cavalry was an Ethiopian from Cerne, perhaps Mogador Island off the Atlantic coast of Morocco.

71. Very little information is available concerning the existence of a trade in black slaves in antiquity. The appearance of Negroes resembling the present inhabitants of Darfur and Kordofan as the prisoners of chieftains in a mural painting in the tomb of Huy (ca. 1342–1333 B.C.) suggests to Vercoutter (*Image of the Black,* p. 63) a hypothesis that he offers with considerable hesitancy: as early as the middle of the second millennium B.C. a trade in slaves from Darfur and Kordofan may have been conducted along routes from the south still in use for a slave trade in the nineteenth century. According to Pliny (*Historia naturalis* 6.34.173) Adule, a two days' sail from Ptolemais on the Red Sea, was a very large emporium of Trogodytes and Ethiopians, a center of trading in slaves and products from inner Africa. Another bit of evidence suggesting a rarely documented trade in black slaves comes from a sixth-century A.D. papyrus—see F. Preisigke, "Ein Sklavenkauf des 6.Jahrhunderts," *Archiv für Papyrusforschung* 3 (1906) 415–424, lines 24–27 of the text of the papyrus on p. 419—pertaining to the sale in the town of Hermopolis of a twelve-year-old girl described as Maura, sold into private ownership by local slave dealers who stated that they had purchased the girl from Ethiopian merchants. See also W. L. Westermann, *The Slave Systems of Greek and Roman Antiquity* (Philadelphia 1955), p. 135.

72. Suetonius *Vita Terenti* 1,5. The earliest references to blacks specifically designated as slaves in Greek and Roman literature illustrate how little information is provided concerning place of origin, physical appearance, and method of acquisition. Theophrastus *Characteres* 21.4 states merely that the man of petty ambition will be pleased only by an Ethiopian attendant, and the *Eunuchus* of Terence (165–167, 470–471) suggests only that a slave girl from Ethiopia is a valuable gift.

3. Images and Attitudes

1. Vercoutter, *Image of the Black,* p. 46.

2. Breasted, *ARE* I, 296, sec. 657.

3. Ibid., 296–297, sec. 659.

4. *ANET,* p. 232.

5. Breasted, *ARE* II, 30, sec. 71.

6. O. W. Muscarella, *Ancient Art: The Norbert Schimmel Collection* (Mainz 1974) no. 202.

7. *Image of the Black,* figs. 55–56; Cairo, Egyptian Museum, JE61467.

8. E. D. Ross, ed., *The Art of Egypt through the Ages* (London 1931) p. 43 and plate 195.

9. *Image of the Black,* fig. 44.

10. Vercoutter, ibid., p. 84.

11. Chapter Four, "The Environment Theory of Racial Differences."

12. *ANET,* p. 370; cf. M. Lichtheim, *Ancient Egyptian Literature: A Book of Readings,* II: *The New Kingdom* (Berkeley 1976) p. 98, and S. Morenz, *Egyptian Religion,* trans. A. E. Keep (Ithaca 1973) pp. 51–52.

13. Trigger, *Nubia under the Pharaohs,* p. 62.

14. E. Riefstahl, "A Wounded Warrior," *Bulletin: The Brooklyn Museum* 16 (1956) 2. For a later example of good feeling toward blacks resulting from military support, compare the French attitude toward Africans after World War I, when black troops had fought on France's behalf. W. B. Cohen, *The French Encounter with Africans: White Response to Blacks, 1530–1880* (Bloomington 1980) pp. 284–285.

15. See Chapter One, note 42.

16. H. E. Winlock, *Excavations at Deir el Bahri, 1911–1931* (New York 1942) p. 130; for a limestone piece from a chapel at Deir el Bahari showing Mentuhotpe embracing a lady of his harem, whose nose and lips suggest Negroid ancestry, see S. Wenig, *The Woman in Egyptian Art* (New York 1969) p. 38 and plate 23.

17. The Prophecy of Neferti, *ANET,* pp. 445–446; *CAH* I, pt. 2, p. 495; and Leclant, *Africa in Antiquity,* p. 64, who points out that Amenemhet's mother was apparently a native of the first nome of Upper Egypt, an area certainly populated by Nubians.

18. Wenig, *The Woman in Egyptian Art,* p. 50, states that the features of Queen Tiy seem to indicate Nubian extraction. A firsthand study of the head (Ägyptisches Museum, West Berlin) strongly suggests to me that the queen was of Negroid admixture. For illustrations of the head, see C. Aldred, *Akhenaten and Nefertiti* (New York 1973) pp. 81 and 105.

19. See Chapter Two, note 19.

20. Kitchen, *Third Intermediate Period,* pp. 381–382, 390.

21. M. Lichtheim, *Ancient Egyptian Literature,* I: *The Old and Middle Kingdoms* (Berkeley 1973) pp. 51–57.

22. Smith, *Interconnections in the Ancient Near East,* p. 5.

23. *ANET,* pp. 294–295.

24. Manetho, as cited by Josephus *Contra Apionem* 1.245–248.

25. Herodotus 2.30; cf. Pliny *Naturalis historia* 6.35.191; Strabo 17.1.2; and Plutarch *de exilio* 601 E; cf. Desanges, *Recherches,* pp. 218–220.

26. Strabo 1.3.21.

27. Diodorus 16.51.1; R. Lane Fox *Alexander the Great* (New York 1974) p. 197.

28. *ANET*, p. 287.

29. *ANET*, p. 292.

30. S. Smith, in chap. 3 (Sennacherib and Esarhaddon) of *CAH* III, 86; cf. A. Spalinger, "The Foreign Policy of Egypt Preceding the Assyrian Conquest," *Chronique d'Egypte* 53 (1978) 22–47.

31. *ANET*, p. 294.

32. Ezekiel 29:10; cf. Isaiah 45:14 and Job 28:19.

33. Isaiah 18:2.

34. Jeremiah 13:23.

35. Isaiah 18:1–2.

36. Numbers 12:1–15. Translations of citations from the Bible are those of *The New English Bible with the Apocrypha* (Oxford and Cambridge 1970).

37. 2 Samuel 18:21, 31–33.

38. Jeremiah 38:6–14, 39:16–18.

39. 2 Chronicles 12:3–9.

40. Isaiah 18:2.

41. 2 Chronicles 14:9–15.

42. 2 Kings 18:19–21; 2 Chronicles 32.9–15.

43. 2 Kings 18:21.

44. Nahum 3:8.

45. Ezekiel 30:4.

46. Zephaniah 3:10.

47. Psalms 68:31.

48. Psalms 87:4–5.

49. Homer *Iliad* 1.423–425, 23.205–207; *Odyssey* 1.22–24; 4.84, 5.282. See A. A. Parry, *Blameless Aegisthus: A Study of AMYMON and other Homeric Epithets, Mnemosyne*, supplement 26 (1973) pp. 156–157, for the basic meaning of *amymon* as referring primarily to bodily beauty and strength, and as acquiring early the connotation of "good" in a nonphysical sense.

50. Hesiod, B. P. Grenfell and A. S. Hunt, *Oxyrhynchus Papyri* 11 (London 1915) no. 1358, Frg. 2, p. 48, col. i, 15–17.

51. Xenophanes, Frg. 16 (Diels).

52. Herodotus 7.70.

53. Ibid. 2.29; cf. Strabo 1.2.25, who refers to Meroë as the metropolis of the Ethiopians; cf. Desanges, *Recherches*, p. 226 and notes 56–57.

54. Herodotus 2.100, 110.

55. Ibid. 2.137, 139.

56. Ibid. 3.20.

57. Ibid. 3.21 (trans. A. D. Godley in Loeb Classical Library).

58. Ibid. 3.25.

59. Ibid. 3.97.

60. E. F. Schmidt, *Persepolis,* I: *Structures, Reliefs, Inscriptions,* University of Chicago Oriental Institute Publications, vol. 68 (Chicago 1953) p. 90 and plate 49; cf. J. Leroy, "Les 'Ethiopiens' de Persépolis," *Annales d' Ethiopie* 5 (1963) 295, who comments on the Negroid nose and hair of the Persepolis Ethiopians.

61. Herodotus 2.106.

62. Ibid. 2.104.

63. Ibid. 2.30.

64. Ibid. 7.69.

65. Aeschylus *Supplices* 154–155.

66. Aeschylus *Prometheus Vinctus* 807–812.

67. For fragments of the *Memnon* and *Psychostasia* of Aeschylus, see A. Nauck, 2nd ed., Frg. 127–130, 279–280; of the *Aethiopes* of Sophocles, Frg. 25–30. Memnon appears as king of the Ethiopians in Hesiod (*Theogony* 984–985) but is described in Callimachus (*Aetia* IV, no. 110, 52–53) as Ethiopian, a designation suggesting that by the time of Callimachus Memnon was regarded as black or Negroid. In the Roman period Memnon was described as black (Vergil *Aeneid* 1.489; Ovid *Amores* 1.8.3–4, Seneca *Agamemnon* 212); cf. Snowden, *Blacks in Antiquity,* pp. 151–154.

68. For fragments of the *Andromeda* of Sophocles, see Nauck, Frg. 122–132; of Euripides, Frg. 114–156. Cf. H. H. Bacon, *Barbarians in Greek Tragedy* (New Haven 1961) esp. pp. 16, 24–26, 89–92, 177–178.

69. For examples of Negroid types in mythological scenes, see the following fifth-century vases depicting the Busiris myth: (1) pelike (Pan Painter) in Athens, National Museum, 9683; (2) stamnos from Vulci, Oxford, Ashmolean Museum, G 270; (3) cup from Vulci, West Berlin, Staatliche Museen, Antikenabteilung, F 2534; (4) cup from Spina, Ferrara, Museo Archeologico Nazionale, 609; (5) stamnos (Altamura Painter), Bologna, Museo Civico Archeologico, 174; *Image of the Black,* figs. 167–169, 171–172. For illustrations of the Andromeda myth: (1) pelike (workshop of the Niobid Painter), Boston, Museum of Fine Arts, 63.2663; (2) calyx-krater, from Capua, East Berlin, Staatliche Museen, Antikenabteilung, 3237; (3) red-figured hydria from Vulci, London, British Museum, E 169; *Image of the Black,* figs. 174–177, and *Blacks in Antiquity,* fig. 26.

70. Inscriptiones Graecae 2^2 no. 1425, col. I, line 25 (p. 38) and no. 1443, col. II, line 117 (p. 58); Pliny *Naturalis historia* 36.4.17; Pausanias 1.33.2–3. Fig. 39 is reproduced in color in *Image of the Black,* fig. 222. See also N. M.

Kontoleon, "The Gold Treasure of Panagurischte," *Balkan Studies* 3 (1962) 191–192.

71. See Chapter Four, note 170.

72. Agatharchides *De Erythraeo Mari* 57–58 GGM I, 147–148; cf. Strabo 16.4.12.

73. Agatharchides *De Erythraeo Mari* 30, GGM I, 129.

74. Ibid. 57, GGM I, 148.

75. Ibid. 51, GGM I, 142.

76. Ibid. 55, GGM I, 146–147.

77. Ibid. 31–49, GGM I, 129–141, for entire account of the Ichthyophagi, and sec. 49 for his moralistic conclusions; cf. P. M. Fraser, *Ptolemaic Alexandria*, II (Oxford 1977) p. 780, n. 187. Some whites, like some blacks, were reported to practice nudity. The inhabitants of the Balearic Islands, according to Diodorus (5.17.1), went naked in the summer, and for that reason the islands were called Gymnesiae. Diodorus (5.30.3) also states that some of the Gauls went into battle naked.

78. Agatharchides *De Erythraeo Mari* 11–20, GGM, pp. 117–119; cf. P. M. Fraser, *Ptolemaic Alexandria*, I (Oxford 1972) pp. 541–542; II, n. 342, pp. 297–298, and n. 179, p. 778; cf. Desanges, *Recherches*, pp. 282–283.

79. Diodorus 3.11. An examination of similarities in Diodorus and Agatharchides shows that the former followed the latter when they discussed the same people. It is likely, therefore, that Diodorus was also drawing to some extent from Agatharchides and was reflecting Ptolemaic knowledge, when Agatharchides is not available for comparison.

80. Diodorus 3.8.5; 3.15.2; 3.9.2.

81. Ibid. 3.8.3.

82. Ibid. 3.34.7–8.

83. Ephorus, cited in Strabo 7.3.9.

84. Diodorus 3.11.

85. Ibid. 3.2–3.7.

86. Pliny *Naturalis historia* 5.8.46; 6.35.188. Gaius Iulius Solinus in his *Collectanea rerum memorabilium* records similar descriptions, taken largely from Pliny, of Garamantian Ethiopians, coastal Ethiopians, Pamphagi, and Anthropophagi. See T. Mommsen's second edition (Berlin 1958) of Solinus, 30.2,4,6,7; 31.5.

87. Ibid 6.3.194,195. See below, notes 123–126, for the well-attested tradition of Ethiopian skill with the bow. Pliny locates peoples in the north, especially in Scythia and beyond, who in several instances are remarkably parallel to his fabulous inhabitants of Africa: Scythian Anthropophagi; Arimaspi, who have one eye in the center of their forehead; the people of Abarimon, who have feet turned backward and who run fast through the

forests like wild beasts (4.12.88; 6.20.53, 7.2.10–12). It is noteworthy that the ancients, unlike later accounts of Africa, did not stereotype blacks as cannibals. Classical literature makes a few references to Ethiopian Anthropophagi (e.g. Pliny 6.3.195; Philostratus *Vita Apollonii* 6.25; Solinus 30.7; Origen *De principiis* 2.9.5, *Die griechischen christlichen Schriftsteller der ersten drei Jahrhunderte* [hereafter *CGS*], Origen 5.169–170. Whites, however, were also reported to have been Anthropophagi—Scythians and other northerners (e.g. Herodotus 4.100, 106, according to whom the manners of the northerners were said to be more savage than those of any other race; Pliny *Naturalis historia* 4.12.88, 6.20.53, 7.2.9, 11–12; Strabo 4.5.4). Strabo's inhabitants of Ierne (Ireland), however (although Strabo adds that he has no reliable witnesses), were among the most "savage" in the ancient world; more savage than the Britons, they considered it honorable to devour their fathers when they died and had intercourse with their mothers and sisters. Other whites, forced by sieges or other dire circumstances, are also reported to have resorted to human flesh (Cambyses' soldiers, Herodotus 3.25; Potidaeans, Thucydides 2.70; Celts and Iberians, Strabo 4.5.4). Two recent books dealing with the image of blacks in later European societies mention certain concepts of Ethiopians found in the classical world—W.B. Cohen, *The French Encounter with Africans: White Response to Blacks, 1530–1880* (Bloomington 1980), and J. B. Friedman, *The Monstrous Races in Medieval Art and Thought* (Cambridge, Mass. 1981). Both studies refer to the monstrous Ethiopians of Pliny or Solinus, Cohen (pp. 1–2) and Friedman (pp. 12, 15, 17, 19). Their failure, however, to include the total "Ethiopian" image gives a distorted picture of the Greco-Roman view of blacks available to readers of Pliny and Solinus. Solinus (30.9–10), for example, mentions the frequently noted justice and handsomeness of the Macrobian Ethiopians (cf. Herodotus, 3.20–21), and Pliny refers to the wisdom of the Ethiopians (2.80.189) and to their fame and power among Mediterranean peoples (6.35.182). In later societies, readers of Pliny, Solinus, and other classical authors dealing with Ethiopians, it should be emphasized, had access to a balanced picture of blacks and to the classical view that certain peoples, both black and white, inhabiting the fringes of the earth were physically bizarre. See J. P. V. D. Balsdon, *Romans and Aliens* (London 1979), p. 59. Further, it should be noted that both Pliny (7.12.51) and Solinus (1.79), in their accounts of the transmission of physical characteristics in the offspring of black-white crosses, report nothing strange about the physical appearance of Nicaeus, the famous Ethiopian boxer from Byzantium, whose mother was born of a black-white union.

88. Pliny *Naturalis historia* 2.80.189; see Plutarch *Septem sapientium convivium* 151 b-c for a contest in wisdom between Amasis, king of the

Egyptians, and a king of the Ethiopians.

89. Lucian *De astrologia* 3–5.

90. Heliodorus *Aethiopica* 4.12.

91. Strabo 1.3.21; 15.1.6.

92. Diodorus 1.65.1; cf. 1.1.60, for Actisanes, perhaps a double of Sabacos.

93. Seneca *De ira* 3.20.2.

94. *Monumentum Ancyranum* 5.26.18–22.

95. M. I. Rostovtzeff, *The Social and Economic History of the Hellenistic World* (Oxford 1941) II, 900, and plate CI, fig. 2; *Allard Pierson Museum, Algemeene Gids* (Amsterdam 1937) p. 50, no. 465, and plate 25; Alexandria, Graeco-Roman Museum, 23099, 19505, 23211.

96. Vergil *Aeneid* 1.488–489.

97. Pliny *Naturalis historia* 6.35.182.

98. Josephus *Antiquitates Judaicae* 2.252–254; cf. Numbers 12:1–16.

99. Ibid. 8.254; cf. 2 Chronicles 12:2–12; 1 Kings 14:25–27.

100. Ibid. 8.292–294; cf. 2 Chronicles 14:9–14.

101. Ibid. 10.15–17; cf. 2 Kings 19:9–13.

102. Ibid. 8.165; cf. 1 Kings 10:1–13; 2 Chronicles 9:1–12.

103. Ibid. 10.122–123; cf. Jeremiah 38.5–13; 39:15–18.

104. See Chapter Four, notes 217, 220, 245–246.

105. See Chapter Two, notes 47–48.

106. Heliodorus *Aethiopica* 9.20; c.f. G. N. Sandy, *Heliodorus* (Boston 1982) pp. 1–5.

107. Ibid. 9.21.

108. Vergil *Aeneid* 6.853.

109. Heliodorus *Aethiopica* 9.27.

110. Ibid. 9.26.

111. Ibid. 10.39.

112. See above, notes 67, 96.

113. Quintus of Smyrna 2.26–32.

114. Ibid. 2.100–112.

115. Ibid. 2.215–216, 355–356.

116. Ibid. 2.614–647.

117. J. Ferguson, *Utopias of the Classical World* (Ithaca 1975) pp. 11–13, 16–22.

118. Homer *Odyssey* 19.246–248.

119. Herodotus 2.137, 139, and above, note 21. For another interesting example of the account of a classical author strikingly confirmed by inscriptional evidence, see the inscription, dating shortly after 600 B.C., found at Gebel Barkal (near Napata) on the divine nomination of an Ethiopian

king (*ANET*, pp. 447–448), which in general conforms to the description of Diodorus 3.5.1, who states that Ethiopian priests first choose the most suitable prospects and then permit the god to select the one to be invested with royal power.

120. See Chapter Two, note 26.

121. Herodotus 3.17–18.

122. A. J. Arkell, *A History of the Sudan: From the Earliest Times to 1821*, 2nd ed. (London 1961) p. 150; Wenig, *Africa in Antiquity*, II, 59; cf. Desanges, *Recherches*, p. 231.

123. Herodotus 3.21, 7.69; Agatharchides, *De Mari Erythraeo* 19, *GGM* I, 119, mentions the Ethiopians with large bows and poisoned arrows.

124. Helidorus 9.18. So faultless was the Ethiopian aim, says Heliodorus, that some of their foes who had been struck ran about in disarray with arrows sticking out of their eyes like flutes.

125. See Chapter One, notes 45–46.

126. P. L. Shinnie, *Medieval Nubia*, Sudan Antiquities Pamphlet No. 2 (Khartoum 1954) p. 4; Adams, *Nubia*, pp. 450–451.

127. Lucian *De astrologia* 3.

128. J. Garstang, "Fifth Interim Report on the Excavations at Meroe in Ethiopia," *Annals of Archaeology and Anthropology* (Liverpool) 7 (1944) 4–6.

129. Wenig, *Africa in Antiquity*, II, 75.

130. Diodorus 3.11.3.

4. Toward an Understanding of the Ancient View

1. W. E. B. DuBois, *The Souls of Black Folk: Essays and Sketches* (New York 1965), p. 23.

2. D. B. Saddington, "Race Relations in the Early Roman Empire," in H. Temporini, ed., *Aufstieg und Niedergang der römischen Welt*, II.3 (Berlin 1975) p. 112.

3. On the importance of distinguishing between ethnocentrism and racism, see P. L. van der Berghe, *Race and Racism: A Comparative Perspective* (New York 1967) p. 12, and "Racism," *New Encyclopaedia Britannica* (1976) XV, 360. For the absence of color prejudice in the ancient world in general, see S. Davis, *Race-Relations in Ancient Egypt: Greek, Egyptian, Hebrew, Roman* (London rpt. 1953) p. 54, and van den Berghe, "Racism," pp. 361–362; and in Egypt, J. A. Wilson, in H. and H. A. Frankfort, J. A. Wilson, T. Jacobsen, and W. A. Irwin, *The Intellectual Adventure of Ancient Man: An Essay on Speculative Thought in the Ancient Near East* (Chicago 1946) pp. 33–34, 37.

4. W. den Boer, review of Snowden, *Blacks in Antiquity*, in *Mnemosyne* 24 (1971) 438 [Review of *Blacks in Antiquity* hereafter *RBA*].

5. M. Cebeillac-Gervasoni, *RBA*, in *L'Antiquité classique* 44 (1975) 781–782.

6. B. M. Warmington, *RBA*, in *African Historical Studies* 4 (1971) 386.

7. W. R. Connor, *RBA*, in *Good Reading: Review of Books Recommended by the Princeton University Faculty* 21 (May 1970) 3.

8. C. T. Seltman, "Two Heads of Negresses," *American Journal of Archaeology* 24 (1920), 14.

9. A. Lane, *Greek Pottery*, 3rd ed. (London 1971) p. 55.

10. D. von Bothmer, "A Gold Libation Bowl," *Bulletin of the Metropolitan Museum of Art* 21 (1962–63) 161, finds the Negroes on the Panagjurishte phiale "almost caricatures." See fig. 39a-b, above.

11. See below, "Art and the Somatic Norm Image."

12. G. H. Beardsley, *The Negro in Greek and Roman Civilization: A Study of the Ethiopian Type* (Baltimore 1929) p. 53.

13. G. Steindorff and K. C. Seele, *When Egypt Ruled the East*, rev. K. C. Seele (Chicago 1957) p. 271.

14. Since the figures of black combatants or captives are usually derived from non-Nubian sources, the numbers must be regarded with caution. Sneferu, for example, claimed 7,000 prisoners in his Nubian campaign, *ARE* I, 66, sec. 146. Strabo in his account (17.1.54) of Petronius' Ethiopian campaign states that the Romans forced 30,000 Ethiopians to flee, and Pliny (6.35.186) writes that Meroë used to furnish 250,000 armed men.

15. R. Mauny, *RBA*, in *Journal of African History* 12 (1971) 159; Warmington, *RBA*, p. 385; J. Desanges, "L'Antiquité gréco-romaine et l'homme noir," *Revue des études latines* 48 (1970) 94.

16. Diodorus 3.2–7; on Ethiopians as an element in the motley population of Alexandria, see Dio Chrysostom *Orationes* 32.40; and below, notes 216–226.

17. P. L. van den Berghe, *Race and Racism: A Comparative Perspective* (New York 1967) p. 13.

18. P. Mason, *Race Relations* (New York 1970) p. 147.

19. C. N. Degler, *Neither Black nor White: Slavery and Race Relations in Brazil and the United States* (New York 1971) pp. 99–100; F. Fernandes, "The Weight of the Past," in J. H. Franklin, ed., *Color and Race* (Boston 1968) [hereafter *Color and Race*] p. 282.

20. L. C. Brown, "Color in Northern Africa," in *Color and Race*, pp. 186–194. Brown makes these points: in north Africa the black-white pattern is not comparable to that in the United States; there has never been anything approximating segregation on the basis of color; there has been no

color bar; north Africa, though not color-blind, has not been color-conscious.

21. Ibid., p. 190.

22. W. D. Jordan, *White over Black: American Attitudes toward the Negro, 1550–1812* (Baltimore 1969) p. 6. J. Walvin, *Black and White: The Negro and English Society, 1555–1945* (London 1973) p. 19, states that the African's blackness and nakedness impressed Englishmen deeply and that these two characteristics placed Africans at opposite physical and social poles to Elizabethan Englishmen, with the result that blacks came to be seen as a "dramatic inversion of their most deeply cherished social and cultural values." G. K. Hunter, "Elizabethans and Foreigners," in *Shakespeare in His Own Age,* ed. A. Nicoll [hereafter *Shakespeare Survey*] (1964) XVII, 37–52.

23. Warmington, *RBA,* p. 385.

24. "The second voyage to Guinea ... in the yere 1554. The Captaine whereof was M. John Lok," in Richard Hakluyt, *The Principal Navigations, Voyages, Traffiques, and Discoveries of the British Nation* (London and New York n.d. [Everyman's Library]) IV, 57.

25. Jordan, *White over Black,* pp. 3–34.

26. Walvin, *Black and White,* pp. 5–8, 28.

27. O. and M. F. Handlin, "The Southern Labor System," in R. W. Winks, *Slavery: A Comparative Perspective: Readings on Slavery from Ancient Times to the Present* (New York 1972) p. 49.

28. M. I. Finley, "The Extent of Slavery," ibid., p. 13.

29. W. L. Westermann cited in F. Tannenbaum, *Slave and Citizen: The Negro in the Americas* (New York 1947) p. 110.

30. R. Bastide, "Color, Racism, and Christianity," in *Color and Race,* p. 36.

31. The Earl of Cromer [Evelyn Baring], *Ancient and Modern Imperialism* (London 1910) pp. 140–142. In commenting on the beauty and vitality of blacks in Hellenistic and Roman art, D. B. Davis in his review of *The Image of the Black in Western Art,* vols. 1 and 2 (*New York Review of Books,* Nov. 5, 1981, p. 40), writes that "such individualized and humanistic representations would have been inconceivable in later slave societies founded on the premise of racial inferiority. In late antiquity the image of the black was one expression of the infinite diversity of a common human nature."

32. E. Shils, "Color, the Universal Intellectual Community, and the Afro-Asian Intellectual," in *Color and Race,* p. 2.

33. R. Hallett, *Africa to 1875: A Modern History* (Ann Arbor 1970) p. 82.

34. Isaiah 18:2, Herodotus 2.137, 139; Diodorus 1.65; Megasthenes cited by Strabo 15.1.6.

35. E.g. Herodotus 3.20–21 and Seneca *De ira* 3.20.2.

36. F. and U. Hintze, *Civilizations of the Old Sudan: Kerma, Kush, Christian Nubia* (Amsterdam 1968) p. 27; Hintze, *Africa in Antiquity*, pp. 89–98; Wenig, *Africa in Antiquity*, II, 65–99. Adams, "Ceramics," *Africa in Antiquity*, pp. 129–130.

37. Herodotus 2:29.

38. M. I. Rostovtzeff, *Social and Economic History of the Roman Empire*, rev. P. M. Fraser I (Oxford 1957) pp. 302–305.

39. Diodorus 3.2.1–3.7; Pliny *Naturalis historia* 2.80.189; Plutarch *Septem sapientium convivium* 151 b-c; Lucian *De astrologia* 3.

40. P. Mason, "The Revolt against Western Values," *Color and Race*, pp. 50–51.

41. Cf. Wenig, *Africa in Antiquity*, II, 48–49; cf. Leclant, *Image of the Black*, pp. 89–104.

42. Agatharchides *De Mari Erythraeo* 16 GGM I, 118.

43. G. W. Allport, *The Nature of Prejudice* (Boston 1964) p. 304.

44. A. Marsh, "Awareness of Racial Differences in West African and British Children," *Race* 11.3 (1970) 289–302.

45. D. and C. Livingstone, *Narrative of an Expedition to the Zambesi and its Tributaries and of a Discovery of the Lakes Shirwe and Nyassa, 1858–1864* (New York 1866) p. 199. Cf. the fifteenth-century Venetian explorer Alvise da Cadamosto, who reported that the Negroes in a Senegalese village "touched my hands and limbs and rubbed me with their spittle to discover whether my whiteness was dye or flesh. Finding that it was flesh they were astounded"—in G. R. Crone, *The Voyages of Cadamosto and Other Documents on Western Africa in the Second Half of the Fifteenth Century* (London 1937) p. 49.

46. Marsh, "Awareness of Racial Differences," p. 301.

47. Ibid., pp. 301–302.

48. Ibid., p. 297.

49. Ovid *Metamorphoses* 2.235–236; see below, note 109.

50. A. Dihle, "Zur hellenistischen Ethnographie," in H. Schwabl et al., Fondation Hardt, Entretiens sur l'antiquité classique, vol. 8, *Grecs et barbares: six exposés et discussions* (Vandoeuvres-Genève 1962) pp. 214–215.

51. H. Hoetink, *The Two Variants in Caribbean Race Relations: A Contribution to the Sociology of Segmented Societies*, trans. E. M. Hookykaas (New York 1967) p. 120.

52. Ibid., p. 126.

53. Philostratus *Vita Apollonii* 2.19. If the reading, *hi pudore*, (Detlefsen suggested *Hypsodores*) in Pliny *Naturalis historia* 6.35.90 is correct, Pliny's statement that the Mesanches, an Ethiopian tribe, covered them-

selves with red because they were ashamed of their blackness differs from the usual Greco-Roman view of the somatic norm image (e.g. Philostratus *Vita Apollonii* 2.19 and Sextus Empiricus *Adversus mathematicos* xi.43.) J. Balsdon, *Rome and Aliens* (London 1979) p. 219, suggests that Pliny may have been wrong as to motive but right as to the Ethiopian practice. Herodotus 7.69 provides an explanation of such a custom when he notes that Ethiopians, upon going into battle, painted their bodies half with chalk and half with vermilion.

54. Dio Chrysostom *Orationes* 21.16–17.

55. Sextus Empiricus *Adversus mathematicos* xi.43.

56. Plato *Respublica* 5.474 DE; Lucretius 4.1160–1169; Ovid *Ars amatoria* 2.657–662; *Remedia amoris* 327. Cf. Martial 4.62, 7.13. For a somewhat similar "intermediate" standard of beauty in Jewish thought, see S. W. Baron, *A Social and Religious History of the Jews*, II: *Christian Era: The First Five Centuries*, 2nd ed. (New York and London 1952) p. 238, who points out that Rabbi Ishmael was proud of the fact that Jews were "like an ebony tree," i.e., of an intermediate color, neither as fair as Germans nor as dark as Negroes. The canon of an ideal intermediate color may have influenced the Midrashic interpretation of Noah's curse on Canaan (Genesis 9.25), e.g. *Midrash Rabbah, Genesis (Noach)* xxxvi.7 [p. 293 in Midrash Rabbah I (Genesis), trans. H. Freedman (London 1939)], which states that Ham's seed would be "ugly and dark-skinned." W. D. Jordan, *White over Black: American Attitudes toward the Negro, 1550–1812* (Baltimore 1969) p. 18, contrasts the difference between the Christian and Talmudic-Midrashic interpretation of Noah's curse. The church fathers, Jordan points out, cited the curse in reference to slavery but not to Negroes, whereas Talmudic and Midrashic sources suggested the curse as the origin of blackness in Ham and his descendants. The criterion of an intermediate color appears also in Arabic and Muslim writers: Jāhiz of Basra (ca. 776–869) described inhabitants of cold countries as undercooked, of hot countries as burned; Ibn al-Faqīh (ca. 902/3) stated that the Iraqis were intermediate in color, neither "half-baked dough" like northerners nor "burned crust" like southerners— B. Lewis, *Race and Color in Islam* (New York 1971) pp. 33–34.

57. J. Desanges, "L'Afrique noire et le monde méditerranéen dans l'Antiquité (Éthiopiens et Gréco-romains)" *Revue française d'histoire d'outre-mer* 62.228 (1975), sees an aesthetic prejudice (pp. 410–411) in a sixth-century poem of Luxorius, who contrasts an ugly Garamantian and a pretty Pontic girl (no. 43 in M. Rosenblum, *Luxorius: A Latin Poet among the Vandals* (New York 1961); and sees anti-black sentiment in another poem of Luxorius in praise of a black charioteer (Rosenblum, no. 67) and in a third-century epitaph, found in Egypt (E. Bernand, *Inscriptions métriques*

de l'Egypte gréco-romaine:Recherches sur la poésie épigrammatique des grecs en Egypte [Besançon and Paris 1969] no. 26, pp. 143–147) in which a master memorializes a slave by contrasting his black color and his white soul. D. S. Wiesen, "Juvenal and the Blacks," *Classica et Mediaevalia* 31 (1970) 132–150, interprets some of the same passages cited by Desanges as well as others in Juvenal as indicative of a pejorative view of blacks. Juvenal's juxtaposition of *Aethiopem albus* (2.23), *Gaetulum Ganymedem* (5.59), and *Aethiopem Cycnum* (8.33), for example, is evidence to Wiesen that the Negro in Juvenal is a "kind of insult to nature and nature's proper product—the white man" (p. 143) and proof that the satirist despised the physical being of Negroes and attached "a special stigma to the physical attributes of blacks and finds in them faults which are neither of their own making nor capable of being corrected" (p. 149). For a different view of Juvenal's attitude toward Negroes and other non-Romans, see W. J. Watts, "Race Prejudice in the Satires of Juvenal," *Acta Classica* 19 (1976) 83–104, who believes (p. 86) that Juvenal is more concerned with cultural than physical differences and that (p. 95) the satirist felt no hostility to any one non-Italian group, except perhaps the Egyptians. Cf. J. Ferguson, *Juvenal: The Satires* (New York 1979) pp. 128–129 on 2.23 and p. 211 on 6.600. Juvenal, of course, must be read with caution because he lashes out at all foreigners regardless of the color of their skin.

As a corrective for some modern interpretations of Juvenal, a look at other writers of the early Roman Empire is appropriate. Seneca (*De ira* 3.26.3), for example, observes that the color of the Ethiopian among his own people is not notable and that among the Germans red hair gathered into a knot is not unbecoming a man. And, Seneca adds, apparently rejecting a common Roman view, one is to consider nothing in a man odd which is characteristic of his nation. Martial, Juvenal's contemporary, states (*Spectacula* 3.9–10) that present at the opening of the Colosseum were Sygambrians with their hair twisted in a knot and Ethiopians with their hair twisted in another way. Like this reference, Martial's other mentions of Ethiopians or dark "beauties" are similarly without judgment (e.g. 1.115). What both Desanges and Wiesen overlook in their interpretations is that the passages they cite as evidence of anti-black sentiment merely reflect a somatic norm image, something found in all societies, black included. Juvenal (13.163–173) himself recognizes such a standard when he says that women in Meroë with large breasts (bigger than their fat babies) and Germans with blue eyes and yellow hair (greasy curls twisted into a horn) evoke no astonishment in their own countries because their physical traits are common. Similarly, the satirist adds, no one would laugh at Pygmies in their native land because the whole population is no taller than one foot.

These important points are seldom mentioned in some modern interpretations of attitudes toward blacks in antiquity: (1) The frequent classical references to the extreme fairness, blue eyes, and light hair of northerners are often omitted while the Ethiopian's blackness is pointed out, an emphasis of modern and not of ancient commentators—cf. J. Balsdon, *Romans and Aliens*, p. 215, who refers to something of a Roman "colour prejudice" against palefaced men—i.e., there were whites as well as blacks who did not conform to classical canons. (2) The Greeks and Romans also designated as dark or black peoples other than Ethiopians, such as Egyptians, Indians, Moors, and Garamantes (one of the passages cited above by Wiesen refers to a Gaetulian and one by Desanges to a Garamantian). (3) There were in the ancient world those who questioned the validity of the classical somatic norm image, others who extolled the beauty of blackness (as Luxorius, no. 67 in Rosenblum), and still others who stated their preferences for black beauty.

58. Herodotus 3.20.

59. Philodemus in *Anthologia Palatina* 5.121 (Loeb I.184).

60. Asclepiades, ibid. 5.210 (Loeb I.232).

61. Theocritus 10.26–29.

62. Suetonius *Vita Terenti* 5.

63. Vergil *Eclogues* 10.37–39, 2.16–18.

64. Ovid *Heroides* 15.35–38.

65. Martial 1.115.

66. Luxorius, *Anthologia Latina,* ed. F. "Bücheler and A. Riese, I, fasc. 1 (Leipzig 1894) pp. 277–278, no. 353; trans. Rosenblum, p. 151.

67. Menander, Fragment 612 in A. Koerte, 2nd ed. (Leipzig 1959); Kock, Frg. 533.

68. Agatharchides *De Mari Erythraeo* 16 GGM I, 118.

69. Luxorius, *Anthologia Latina,* 278, no. 354; trans. Rosenblum, pp. 151–153.

70. Ibid., p. 251, no. 293; trans. Rosenblum, pp. 114–115.

71. Propertius 2.25.41–42.

72. See *Image of the Black*, e.g., figs. 169, 176, 197, 275, 286, 334.

73. C. T. Seltman, "Two Heads of Negresses," *American Journal of Archaeology* 24 (1920) 14.

74. W. N. Bates, "Scenes from the Aethiopis on a Black-Figured Amphora from Orvieto," *Transactions of the Department of Archaeology,* University of Pennsylvania Free Museum of Science and Art (Philadelphia 1904) I and II, 50.

75. M. Robertson, *Greek Painting* (Geneva 1959) p. 67.

76. E. Riefstahl, "A Wounded Warrior," *Bulletin: The Brooklyn Mu-*

seum 17.4 (1956) 6, states that it is rare to find Negro types caricatured in Egyptian art of the pharaonic period, and that while Egyptian artists noted carefully the physical features of blacks, they did not regard Negroes as ludicrous or grotesque. For a view of Negroes as caricature, see R. Winkes, "Physiognomonia: Probleme der Charakterinterpretation römischer Porträts," in H. Temporini, ed., *Aufstieg und Niedergang der römischen Welt,* I.4: *Von den Anfängen Roms bis zum Ausgang der Republik* (Berlin and New York 1973) pp. 908–913; and note 10 above. For interpretations of the Negro as comic, see next note.

77. G. H. Beardsley, *The Negro in Greek and Roman Civilization,* pp. 37–38, 39, 47, 65, 81; C. M. Havelock, *Hellenistic Art: The Art of the Classical World from the Death of Alexander the Great to the Battle of Actium* (London 1971) p. 136; *Image of the Black,* fig. 268 and p. 206.

78. R. A. Higgins, *Greek Terracottas* (London 1967) p. 120; *Image of the Black,* figs. 262–263. For a marble head of a Negroid youth of about 100 B.C. in Toronto, which perhaps belonged to a Spinario, see N. Leipen, "Grotesque Head of a Young Man," *Antike Kunst* 23 (1980) pp. 154–158, figs. 1–2, and plates 41–42.

79. H. Read, *A Coat of Many Colours: Occasional Essays* (London 1945) pp. 2, 5. See fig. 28 above and *Image of the Black,* fig. 242.

80. *Image of the Black,* figs. 262–263 and p. 206.

81. A. J. Evans, "Recent Discoveries of Tarentine Terra-Cottas," *Journal of Hellenic Studies* 7 (1886) 37–38; *The Image of the Black,* I, figs. 262–263.

82. D. G. Mitten, *Classical Bronzes: Catalogue of the Classical Collection,* Museum of Art, Rhode Island School of Design (Providence 1975) p. 62. See fig. 24 above and *Image of the Black,* fig. 239.

83. H. Deschamps, *RBA,* in *Africa: Journal of the International African Institute* 41 (1971) p. 68.

84. Cf. G. Becatti, *The Art of Ancient Greece and Rome from the Rise of Greece to the Fall of Rome* (New York 1967) p. 274; D. M. Buitron, "Greek Encounters with Africans," *Walters Art Gallery Bulletin* 32 (Nov. 5, 1980) 1: "In general Greek representations of Ethiopians are of high quality."

85. J. D. Beazley, "Charinos: Attic Vases in the Form of Human Heads," *Journal of Hellenic Studies* 49 (1929) 39.

86. H. Metzger, *RBA,* in *Revue des études anciennes* 73 (1971) 498.

87. J. Neils, "The Group of the Negro Alabastra: A Study in Motif Transferal," *Antike Kunst* 23 (1980) 22.

88. *Image of the Black,* figs. 174–175 and p. 155.

89. See, for example, the footstool decorated with black and Asiatic captives from Thebes, the tomb of Tutankhamun in *Image of the Black,* fig.

37; and the Asiatic (carved in ivory) and black (in ebony) captives bound to the handle of a ceremonial walking stick, also from Tutankhamun's tomb, in E. D. Ross, ed. *The Art of Egypt through the Ages* (London 1931) p. 43 and plate 195.

90. For examples of "pure" Negroes in Andromeda scenes, see *Image of the Black*, figs. 174–175, and for mixed black-white types, see fig. 176; and Snowden, *Blacks in Antiquity*, fig. 26. For illustrations of several Negroid types in the Busiris legend, see *Image of the Black*, figs. 167–173. For late sixth-century kantharoi of conjoined black and white heads, see *Image of the Black*, fig. 160, and *Blacks in Antiquity*, fig. 12. For the frescoes from Herculaneum, see figs. 60–61 below and, in color, *Image of the Black*, figs. 288–289, in which black Isiac cultists are contrasted with white worshipers; the brilliance of the white tunics of the blacks emphasizes the ebony hue of their heads and shoulders.

91. For a Negro Spinario, see above, notes 77–78. The Negro boy in fig. 47 above has been interpreted as an adaptation of the well-known *Boy Blowing a Fire*, of the Hellenistic painter Antiphilus (Pliny, *Historia naturalis* 35.40.138); see K. Herbert, *Greek and Latin Inscriptions in The Brooklyn Museum* (Brooklyn 1972) pp. 14–16 and plate 5. For a capital (second half of the first century B.C.) in the shape of youthful Eros with broad nose, thick lips, and curly hair, found in underwater excavations near Mahdia off the Tunisian coast, see A. Lézine, "La 'Maison des chapiteaux historiés' à Utique," *Karthago* 7 (1956), plates 6–7 and p. 20.

92. D. B. Davis, *The Problem of Slavery in Western Culture* (Ithaca 1966) p. 449. Davis, in his review of the first two volumes of *The Image of the Black in Western Art*, in *New York Review of Books*, considers the pictorial image of blacks from the pharaohs to Emperor Charles V most impressive because of the interest and delight in diversity, the dignity with which artists portrayed most blacks, and their enduring capacity for empathy and human expression; and he concludes that, in spite of the complexities of the black image, "the artistic heritage from Egyptian and Hellenistic times to the great portraits by Memling, Bosch, and Rembrandt presents an unanswerable challenge to the later racist societies that have relied on dehumanizing caricature as an instrument of social and economic oppression" (p. 42).

93. See *melas* and compounds in H. G. Liddell and R. Scott, *A Greek-English Lexicon*, rev. H. S. Jones and R. McKenzie (Oxford 1968), and *niger* and compounds in P. G. W. Glare, *Oxford Latin Dictionary* (Oxford 1976 V, p. 1176; J. André, *Étude sur les termes de couleur dans la langue latine* (Paris 1949) pp. 57, 362–364; A. Hermann, s.v. "Farbe" in T. Klauser, ed.,

Reallexikon für Antike und Christentum, 7 (Stuttgart 1969) cols. 358–447; E. Irwin, *Colour Terms in Greek Poetry* (Toronto 1974) pp. 158–193.

94. K. J. Gergen, "The Significance of Skin Color in Human Relations," in *Color and Race,* pp. 120, 112–125; for examples of recent studies on the colors black and white and for the findings cited, see also Davis, *The Problem of Slavery,* pp. 447–452; Jordan, *White over Black,* pp. 4–20; Degler, *Neither Black nor White,* pp. 207–211; J. E. Williams and J. K. Morland, *Race, Color, and the Young Child* (Chapel Hill 1976) pp. 33–45; D. Zahan, "White, Red and Black; Colour Symbolism in Black Africa," in A. Portmann and R. Ritsema, eds., *The Realms of Colour* (Leiden 1974) pp. 365–396, esp. 364, 373.

95. Degler, *Neither Black nor White,* p. 211.

96. Appian *Bella civilia* 4.17.134; Florus 2.17.7.7–8; Plutarch *Brutus* 48.

97. Suetonius *Caligula* 57.4.

98. SHA, *Septimius Severus* 22.4–5.

99. *Anthologia Latina,* I, fasc. 1, no. 183, pp. 155–156.

100. For *niger Jupiter* and *niger Dis,* see Seneca *Hercules Oetaeus* 1705; Statius *Thebais* 2.49, 4.291; Ovid *Metamorphoses* 4.438.

101. Vergil *Aeneid* 6.298–299.

102. *Aeneid* 6.128, 134–135, 298–299.

103. Gergen, "The Significance of Skin Color," p. 121.

104. For examples of the environment theory in the early empire, see Diodorus 3.34.7–8; Pliny, *Naturalis historia* 2.80.189; Vitruvius *De architectura* 6.1.3–4; Ptolemy *Tetrabiblos* 2.2.56. Illustrations of "just" Ethiopians in the early empire appear in Diodorus 3.2.2–3.3.1; Seneca *De ira* 3.20.2; Pausanias 1.33.4; Heliodorus *Aethiopica* 9.21, 26; 10.39. See also "Christianity" later in this chapter.

105. Xenophanes Frg. 16 (Diels); *The Image of the Black,* figs. 159–160, and above, Chapter One, note 62.

106. Hippocrates *Aër.* xii, xvii–xxiv.

107. Hippocrates *Vict.* 2:37.

108. Polybius 4.20–21.

109. Pliny *Naturalis historia* 2.80.189.

110. Polybius 4.20–21; Diodorus 3.34.7–8. For the advantage of the ideal intermediate climate of Greece and Italy, see Vitruvius 6.1.11; Strabo 6.4.1; Ptolemy *Tetrabiblos* 2.56–57; Galen *De sanitate tuenda* 2.7.

111. Achilles Tatius 4.5.2; Lucian *Bis accusatus* 6.

112. Lucian *Adversus indoctum* 28; cf. *Anthologia Palatina* 11.428 (ascribed to Lucian) which uses *Indikon* instead of *Aithiopikon* in a variation of the proverb.

113. Dio Cassius 46.55.5; Martial *Spectacula* 3.9–10; Juvenal 13.164–165; Tacitus *Germania* 38.

114. Seneca *De ira* 3.26.3 (trans. H. W. Basore in Loeb Classical Library).

115. Pliny *Naturalis historia* 7.1.6.

116. Lucian *Hermotimus* 31.

117. Menander, *Fragment* 533 (Kock).

118. See below, "Christianity."

119. A. Toynbee, *A Study of History* (London and New York 1935) I, 250, 252–253.

120. See *Image of the Black*, figs. 239, 253–255, 266, 269–270, 275–277; Snowden, *Blacks in Antiquity*, figs. 42, 109–110, 113–114.

121. See note 81 above.

122. See also *Image of the Black*, figs. 253–255 and p. 199.

123. M. B. Comstock and C. C. Vermeule, *Sculpture in Stone: The Greek, Roman, and Etruscan Collections of the Museum of Fine Arts, Boston*, no. 339 (Boston 1974) pp. 214–215; *Romans and Barbarians*, exhibition dates, December 17, 1976–February 27, 1977, no. 11 (Department of Classical Art, Museum of Fine Arts Boston, 1976) p. 9.

124. P. M. Fraser, *Ptolemaic Alexandria* (Oxford 1972) I, 74; Adams, *Nubia*, pp. 61–62.

125. Wilson, *Intellectual Adventure of Ancient Man*, pp. 33–34.

126. H. Frankfort, *The Birth of Civilization in the Near East* (Bloomington 1951) p. 90.

127. Ibid. and D. O'Connor, "Ancient Egypt and Black Africa—Early Contacts," *Expedition: The Magazine of Archaeology/Anthropology* 14 (1971) 9.

128. Alexandria, Graeco-Roman Museum, 3204; Snowden, *Blacks in Antiquity*, fig. 71.

129. Sidonius *Carmina* 5.460.

130. M. Launey, *Recherches sur les armées hellénistiques*, Bibliothèque des Ecoles Françaises d'Athènes et de Rome VI (Paris 1949) I, 59–60, 598.

131. See also *Image of the Black*, figs. 251–252.

132. Diodorus interviewed Ethiopian ambassadors resident in Egypt (Diodorus 3.11.3).

133. *Image of the Black*, fig. 280.

134. Cf. Eusebius *De vita Constantini* 4.7, *GCS*, Eusebius I, p. 120.

135. Strabo 17.3.7.

136. See also *Image of the Black*, fig. 350.

137. Ibid., fig. 340. The iconographical evidence for the presence of blacks in Roman northwest Africa has not received the attention it deserves. Desanges (*Image of the Black*, pp. 258, 260) has properly noted that Nilotic scenes and certain Hellenistic themes in north African art cannot be considered as reflections of daily reality. Even though a scene such as that of the black musicians on a second-century mosaic from Lepcis Magna (*Image of the Black*, fig. 346) may owe its inspiration to a traditional theme, the craftsman may have found his models among local blacks. M. I. Rostovtzeff, *The Social and Economic History of the Roman Empire*, 2nd ed. rev. P. M. Fraser, I (Oxford 1957), in his descriptions of plates 62 and 63 (pp. 328–329) has called attention to the important information that mosaics have provided for the reconstruction of life in Roman north Africa. In spite of the traditional element, especially in the art of the first two centuries A.D., mosaicists in the third century and later often demonstrated an interest in the life about them. The details of many of these mosaics seem to portray with fidelity the life of town and country and in a number of instances provide important testimony as to the physical type of blacks in the north African population, the regions in which they lived, and their role in the society. E. Waywell, in a review of K. M. D. Dunbabin, *The Mosaics of Roman North Africa: Studies in Iconography and Patronage* in *Classical Review* 30 (1980) 115, points out that although traditional mythological themes never disappeared, new African subjects revealing an increased interest in the authentic portrayal of north African life became more popular.

138. S. Aurigemma, *L'Italia in Africa: Le Scoperte archeologiche (1911–1943)*, *Tripolitania*, I: *I Monumenti d'arte decorativa, I mosaici* (Rome 1960) p. 44 and plate 70.

139. See also *Image of the Black*, fig. 355.

140. The hunt mosaic from Hippo Regius, Annaba, Musée; *Image of the Black*, fig. 361.

141. P. Gauckler, *Inventaire des mosaïques de la Gaule et de l'Afrique: Tome deuxième: Afrique Proconsulaire [Tunisie]* (Paris 1910) p. 256, no. 764.

142. Mosaic from baths at Timgad, Timgad, Musée Archéologique; *Image of the Black*, fig. 347. For blacks as bath attendants elsewhere, see *Rhetorica ad Herennium* 4.50.63; Pompeiian mosaic of first century from entrance to the *caldarium* of the House of the Menander, A. Maiuri, *La Casa del Menandro e il suo tesoro di argenteria* (Rome 1933) I, 146–147 and fig. 68; *Image of the Black*, fig. 284.

143. See fig. 26 above; J. W. Salomonson, ed., *Mosaïques romaines de Tunisie: Catalogue* no. 29 (Brussels 1964) pp. 33–34, 178.

144. Mosaic from Thysdrus of scenes from the amphitheater, Sousse,

Musée de Sousse; Gauckler, *Inventaire des mosaïques de la Gaule et de l'Afrique*, p. 15, no. 71; L. Foucher, *Guide du Musée de Sousse* (Tunis 1967) p. 31 and fig. 39.

145. For the gladiator, see Carthage, Musée National du Bardo, 899.1; S. Deneauve, "Terres cuites de l'Afrique romaine," *Mélanges de Carthage* 10 (1964–65), 132, plate IV, fig. 2. Though Deneauve describes the nose as flat and the hair as curly, he does not mention that the figure is obviously Negroid.

146. Carthage, Antiquarium; J. W. Salomonson, *La Mosaïque aux chevaux de l'Antiquarium de Carthage* (The Hague 1965) I, 95–96 and tableau 4, plate 58, fig. 2.

147. Sousse, Musée de Sousse, 19; L. Foucher, *Inventaire des mosaïques, Feuille no. 57 de l'Atlas Archéologique* (Tunis 1960) pp. 94–95, plates XLIX, no. 57.211; *idem, Guide du Musée de Sousse* (Tunis 1967) p. 25 and fig. 23.

148. See also *Image of the Black*, fig. 349.

149. See above, note 70. For other Negro or mixed types as grooms or jockeys, see the Negroid groom wearing a fillet in his hair on an Attic red-figure cup (ca. 480 B.C.) attributed to Onesimus, in Muscarella, *Ancient Art: The Norbert Schimmel Collection*, no. 60; the young black groom (in marble) steadying a horse, from Athens, late fourth or early third century B.C., Athens National Museum, 4464; mulatto groom (in marble), late fourth century B.C., fragment of a funerary relief, Copenhagen, Ny Carlsberg Glyptotek, IN 2807; and the bronze of the mixed black-white jockey (late third or early second century B.C.) from Cape Artemisium, Athens, National Museum, 15177; *Image of the Black*, figs. 231–233, 275.

150. See also R. Massigli, *Musée de Sfax*, 17 Musées de l'Algérie et de la Tunisie, no. 17 (Paris 1912) p. 9, no. 24, and plate 5, no. 3; Yacoub, *Guide du Musée de Sfax*, p. 44 and plate 14, figs. 2–3.

151. *CIL* VIII.11824 (Dessau, *ILS* 7457); Rostovtzeff, *Social and Economic History of the Roman Empire*, I, 331.

152. On the role of the national *numeri* and of the Mauri as elite units in the first three centuries A.D., see M. P. Speidel, "The Rise of Ethnic Units in the Roman Imperial Army," in *Aufstieg und Niedergang der römischen Welt: Geschichte und Kultur Roms im Spiegel der neueren Forschung*, H. Temporini, ed., II.3 (Berlin and New York 1975) pp. 202–231; SHA, *Septimius Severus* 22.4–5; H. P. L'Orange, "Maurische Auxilien im Fries des Konstantinsbogens," *Symbolae Osloenses* 13 (1934) 105–113, and "Una strana testimonianza finora inosservata nei rilievi del'Arco di Costantino: Guerrieri etiopici nelle armate imperiali romane," *Roma: Rivista di studi e di vita romana* 14 (1936) 217–222.

153. See Chapter Two, note 68.

154. Isocrates *Panegyricus* 50.

155. P. L. Shinnie, *Meroe: A Civilization of the Sudan* (New York 1967) p. 23.

156. Diodorus 3.6.3; cf. Heliodorus *Aethiopica* 9.25 for the statement that the kings of Ethiopia studied Greek.

157. Comstock and Vermeule, *Greek, Etruscan, and Roman Bronzes in the Museum of Fine Arts, Boston*, pp. 78–79, and *Image of the Black*, fig. 259. In view of the resemblance between the pose of the boy and that of the Epicurean Hermachus in New York, Comstock and Vermeule suggest that the youth may have studied at one of the schools of Epicurus.

158. Acts 8.26–40.

159. Bernand, *Inscriptions métriques de l' Egypte gréco-romaine*, pp. 591–610. I agree with those who interpret *barbariken lexin* of line 24 (p. 593) as referring to the speech of Maximus and not that of Mandulis. The suggestions that the word "Ethiopians" was applied to Egyptians and that Maximus as a Nubian could not have acquired the Greek culture evident in the poem are not supported by the ancient evidence. See Bernand, pp. 606–607, and H. Weil, "Un Poète éthiopien," *Études de littérature et de rythmique grecques* (Paris 1902) pp. 112–119; A. D. Nock, "A Vision of Mandulis Aion," *Harvard Theological Review* 27 (1934) 53, 59–60; O. Guéraud, "La Stèle gréco-démotique de Moschion," *Bulletin de la Société Royale d'Archéologie-Alexandrie*, no. 31 (1937) p. 187; C. Préaux, "De la Grèce classique à l' Egypte hellénistique: Traduire ou ne pas traduire," *Chronique d'Egypte* 42 (1967) 373.

160. Diogenes Laertius 2.86; 10.25. (I am grateful to Werner A. Krenkel of the University of Rostock for this reference.)

161. Neda Leipen of the Royal Ontario Museum, Toronto, to whom I am grateful for allowing me access to her manuscript scheduled to appear in *Antike Plastik* (edited by F. Eckstein), interprets this Negroid figure as one of the "philosophers" or "sages" popular on the sarcophagi of the muses in the third century.

162. On the question of the race of Terence, described by Suetonius as *colore fusco* (dark) (*Vita Terenti* 5), see Snowden, *Blacks in Antiquity*, p. 270, n. 3.

163. See also *Image of the Black*, figs. 363–364 and p. 265. See G. M. A. Richter, *The Portraits of the Greeks* III (Phaidon 1965) figs. 2007–2008, for another portrait of Juba in the Louvre (MA 1886). E. Boucher-Colozier, "Quelques marbres de Cherchel au Musée du Louvre," *Libyca: Archéologie—Epigraphie* I (1953) pp. 23–28, calls attention to the thick lips and curly

hair of a head of Juba II in the Louvre and the skull of Negroid type in the Cherchell Museum.

164. Philostratus *Vita Apollonii* 3.11 and *Vita Sophistarum* 2.588; P. Graindor, *Un Milliardaire antique: Hérode Atticus et sa famille* (Cairo 1930) pp. 114–116, 131, 154, 228; *Image of the Black*, figs. 366–368.

165. Degler, *Neither Black nor White*, p. 212.

166. Lycophron *Alexandra* 535–537. See R. Carden, *The Papyrus Fragments of Sophocles* (Berlin and New York 1974), pp. 52–59, 70–71, for his interpretation of E. Lobel *Oxyrhynchus Papyri* (London 1956) XXIII, 2369, frg. i, col. ii 26. Cf. R. Seaford, "Black Zeus in Sophocles' *Inachus*," *Classical Quarterly*, n.s., 30 (1980) pp. 23–29.

167. Aeschylus *Prometheus Vinctus* 851; Hesiod, ed. B. P. Grenfell and A. S. Hunt *Oxyrhynchus Papyri* XI (London 1915) no. 1358, frg. 2, 15–17.

168. Aeschylus *Supplices* 154–155; Apollodorus *Bibliotheca* 2.1.5.

169. A. Diller, *Race Mixture among the Greeks before Alexander* (Westport, Conn. 1971) p. 43.

170. See *Image of the Black*, figs. 187–192 and pp. 161, 164, and F. M. Snowden, Jr., "AITHIOPES," in *Lexicon Iconographicum Mythologiae Classicae* I.1 (Zurich and Munich 1981) pp. 413–419; and I.2 (Plates) pp. 321–326.

171. Ovid *Amores* 1.13.33–34; cf. H. Fraenkel, *Ovid: A Poet between Two Worlds* (Berkeley and Los Angeles 1945) pp. 14, 178.

172. For Andromeda's dark color, see *Heroides* 15.35–36; *Ars Amatoria* 1.53, 3.191; cf. *Metamorphoses* 4.669. For Andromeda as white, see Philostratus *Imagines* 1.29, Achilles Tatius 3.7.4; and Heliodorus *Aethiopica* 4.8; and her father as a mulatto, see H. Hoffmann, "Attic Red-figured Pelike from the Workshop of the Niobid Painter, ca. 460 B.C.," *Bulletin of the Museum of Fine Arts, Boston* XVI (1963) p. 108; A. D. Trendall and T. B. L. Webster, *Illustrations of Greek Tragedy* (London 1971) pp. 63–65 and fig. III, 2.2; *Image of the Black*, figs. 174–175.

173. See above, Chapter One, note 42.

174. S. Wenig, *The Woman in Egyptian Art* (New York 1969), p. 50, states that the features of Queen Tiy seem to indicate Nubian extraction. A firsthand study of the head (no. 21834, "Ägyptisches Museum, West Berlin) suggests to me strongly that the queen was of Negroid mixture. See fig. 19, pp. 81 and 105, in C. Alfred, *Akhenaten and Nerfertiti* (New York 1973) for illustrations of the head.

175. See above, Chapter One, note 45; Herodotus 2.30.

176. Numbers 12; Josephus *Antiquitates Judaicae* 2.252–253.

177. Suetonius *Vita Terenti* 5.

178. Asclepiades *Anthologia Palatina* 5.210; Martial 1.115.4–5.

179. *CIL* IV 1520, 1523, 1526, 1528, 1536, 6892, Snowden, *Blacks in Antiquity*, p. 321, no. 72, and p. 328, n. 149.

180. Aristotle *De generatione animalium* 1.18.722a; *Historia animalium* 7.6.585b.

181. Plutarch *De sera numinis vindicta* 21(563).

182. Martial 6.39.6–7, and 18; Juvenal 6.595–601.

183. Jerome *Hebraicae quaestiones in Genesim* 30, 32.33 CCL 72.38.

184. Heliodorus *Aethiopica* 4.8; cf. Calpurnius Flaccus *Declamationes* 2 (ed. G. Lehnert [Leipzig 1903]) for a declamation "Natus Aethiopus," which considered the question of whether a white mother to whom a black child was born was guilty of adultery.

185. Numbers 12; Josephus *Antiquitates Judaicae* 2.252–253.

186. R. Sanders, *Lost Tribes and Promised Lands: The Origins of American Racism* (Boston 1978) p. 48.

187. See H. Hoetink, *The Two Variants in Caribbean Race Relations: A Contribution to the Sociology of Segmented Societies*, trans. E. M. Hooykaas (London and New York 1967) p. 186, and *Slavery and Race Relations in the Americas: Comparative Notes on their Nature and Nexus* (New York and London 1973), pp. 187–188, for the estimates that non-whites in Puerto Rico have been halved in the last century, and that in Argentina the black and colored elements, which in 1852 numbered 125,000 out of a population of 816,000 and constituted thirty-four percent of the population of Buenos Aires, have completely disappeared as a social group.

188. L. C. Brown, "Color in Northern Africa," in *Color and Race*, pp. 191–194.

189. Hoetink, *Slavery and Race Relations in the Americas*, p. 113. The existence of the social racial continuum, Hoetink points out, has led some specialists to believe that social, not racial, prejudice exists in Latin America.

190. Apuleius *Metamorphoses* 11.4; for Isis and black cultists, see F. M. Snowden, Jr., "Ethiopians and the Isiac Worship," *Antiquité classique*, 25.1 (1956) 112–116; *Blacks in Antiquity*, pp. 191–192, *Image of the Black*, pp. 221–224; and Leclant, *Image of the Black*, pp. 282–285. Both Strabo 17.3.822 and Diodorus 3.9 mention Isis as one of the deities venerated by the Ethiopians.

191. Priscus 21 *Fragmenta Historicorum Graecorum*, IV 100–101; cf. J. B. Bury, *History of the Later Roman Empire: From the Death of Theodosius I to the Death of Justinian*, A.D. 395 to A.D. 565 (London 1923) II, 371.

192. Procopius *De bello Persico* 1.19.37.

193. R. E. Witt, *Isis in the Graeco-Roman World* (London 1971) pp. 61–63, Adams, *Nubia*, pp. 337–338; F. Dunand, *Le Culte d'Isis dans le bassin*

oriental de la Méditerranée, I: *Le Culte d'Isis et les Ptolemées* (Leiden 1973) pp. 150–161, 195, 205; E. Bernand, *Les Inscriptions grecques de Philae,* II: *Haut et Bas Empire* (Paris 1969) pp. 127–138, 192–197.

194. See also M. Malaise, *Inventaire préliminaire des documents égyptiens découverts en Italie* (Leiden 1972), pp. 251–252, plate 35; *Image of the Black,* fig. 288.

195. Malaise, *Inventaire,* pp. 252–253, plate 36; *Image of the Black,* fig. 289. D. Bonneau, *La Crue du Nil (Divinité égyptienne à travers mille ans d'histoire (332 av.–641 ap. J. C.): Etudes et commentaires* (Paris 1964) p. 520, suggests that the central figure was a priest dressed as the Nile.

196. Malaise, *Inventaire,* pp. 58–59, plate 2; *Image of the Black,* figs. 383–384.

197. Witt, *Isis in the Graeco-Roman World,* p. 22.

198. Apuleius *Metamorphoses* 11.26.

199. Origen, *De principiis* 2.9.5–6 (trans. Rufinus), *GCS,* Origen 5.164–170.

200. Venantius Fortunatus *Carmina* 5.2.7–10 in *Monumenta Germaniae Historica* IV (Auctores Antiquissimi) pt. 1, p. 104.

201. The most comprehensive treatment of the Ethiopian in early patristic writings is the indispensable study of J. M. Courtès, "The Theme of 'Ethiopia' and 'Ethiopians' in Patristic Literature," pp. 9–32, in J. Devisse, *The Image of the Black in Western Art, II: From the Early Christian Era to the "Age of Discovery,"* 1, *From the Demonic Threat to the Incarnation of Sainthood* (New York 1979). For another detailed study of the "Ethiopian" theme in classical and later periods, see also L. Cracco Ruggini, "Il negro buono e il negro malvagio del mondo classico," pp. 108–135 and the bibliography cited, in *Contributi dell'Istituto di Storia Antica* (Pubblicazioni dell'Universita Cattolica del Sacro Cuore, Milano VI, 1979).

202. P. Prigent and R. A. Kraft, *Épître de Barnabe* 4.10, 20.1, *Sources chrétiennes,* no. 172 (Paris 1971) pp. 100–101, 210–211.

203. *Vie de Sainte Mélanie* 54, ed. D. Gorce, *Sources chrétiennes* no. 90 (Paris 1962) pp. 234–235.

204. Didymus the Blind, *In Zachariam* 4.312, ed. L. Doutreleau, *Sources chrétiennes,* no. 85 (Paris 1962) pp. 964–965. F. J. Dölger, *Die Sonne der Gerechtigkeit und der Schwarze: Eine religionsgeschichtliche Studie zum Taufglöbnis* (Münster 1918), contains some of the major references in classical and early Christian literature to black devils and demons, pp. 49–57; to black and evil, pp. 57–64; to the devil and black Zeus, pp. 64–75. J. B. Russell's chapter on evil in the classical world, *The Devil: Perceptions of Evil from Antiquity to Primitive Christianity* (Ithaca 1977) pp. 122–173, makes pertinent observations on the concept of blackness in Greek and Roman literature. On p. 247 Russell points out that nowhere

does the New Testament describe Satan as actually black, and that only in the Apocryphal literature is blackness specifically assigned to the devil. The blackness of the devil, according to Russell, is a natural development from his role "of lord of darkness in opposition to the Kingdom of God and from his association with the underworld or pit where he is imprisoned after his fall."

205. Palladius, *Historia Lausiaca* 2 (*PL* 74:347), an Ethiopian girl picking corn; *Vitae Patrum* 5.5 (*PL* 73.879), an Ethiopian woman, foul-smelling and unsightly; *Actus Petri cum Simone* 22 in R. A. Lipsius and M. Bonnet, *Acta Apostolorum Apocrypha* (Leipzig 1891) p. 70, a most unsightly woman in appearance "most Ethiopian, not Egyptian, but altogether black"; Rufinus, *Historia Monachorum* 29 (*PL* 21.454), tiny, repulsive Ethiopian boys; John Moschus, *Pratum Spirituale* 160 (*PL* 74.200), a dancing Ethiopian boy; John Moschus, *Pratum Spirituale* 66 (*PL* 74.160), an Ethiopian man of extraordinary size.

206. *Passio Sanctarum Perpetuae et Felicitatis* 10 in H. Musurillo, *The Acts of the Christian Martyrs: Introduction, Texts, and Translations* (Oxford 1972) pp. 116–118, the devil in the form of an Egyptian of vicious appearance; John Moschus, *Pratum Spirituale* 105 (*PL* 74.171), demons in the shape of two crows; *Vita beati Antonii Abbatis* 4 (*PL* 73.130), a grim black boy.

207. *Actus Petri cum Simone* 22 and Chapter One, notes 14–19.

208. Courtès, "The Theme of 'Ethiopia,' " pp. 9, 19.

209. Bugner, *Image of the Black*, p. 14, notes that in later iconography the symbolism of blackness was generally employed without using Negroid features in depicting demons, and he considers it remarkable that, in view of the abundant use of the demoniac comparison in texts from the earliest times of the church, we find so few demons with the features of blacks.

210. Although Courtès, "The Theme of 'Ethiopia,' " p. 10, notes that the demonological texts "resolutely avoid any contact with the realities of anthropology," and points out (p. 19) that the comparisons of evil spirits and Ethiopians bear no real resemblance to actual Ethiopians, he states that "while the Ethiopians were in no sense relegated to spiritual ostracism, they suffered nonetheless by their metaphorical relationship with the demons, and their small number in the midst of white society kept more favorable evidence from making itself felt" (p. 21). This conclusion, in my judgment, is supported neither by the ancient evidence nor by the findings of the social sciences: (1) Courtès points out that the demonological texts were limited in scope; (2) the formidable exegetical interpretations from Origen to the sixth century leave no doubt about the equality of the Ethiopian in the eyes of the exegetes; (3) the black population in the ancient world, especially in Egypt, was larger than Courtès implies (see Devisse, *Image of the*

Black, II, pt. 1, p. 38, who mentions the large black population living side by side with whites in Egypt prior to the seventh century). Interpretations that consider the black-white imagery in classical and early Christian texts as a source of color prejudice should be reexamined in the light of modern findings. K. J. Gergen, "The Significance of Skin Color in Human Relations," *Color and Race*, p. 121, for example, raises the question whether individuals who react negatively to the color black have antipathy toward dark-skinned people, and he considers the evidence far from conclusive. In view of the overall attitude toward blacks in antiquity, it is highly unlikely that large numbers of whites acquainted with the black-white imagery would have regarded Ethiopians themselves as demoniacal, diabolical, or evil.

211. Some of the key passages in Origen's "Ethiopian" exegesis appear in *Commentarium in Canticum Canticorum* 2.360–380, *GCS* (Origen 8.113–127) and *Homiliae in Canticum* 1.6 *GCS* (Origen 8.35–38).

212. The Song of Songs 1:5 reads, "I am black and (*kai*) beautiful" in the Septuagint; Origen *Commentarium in Canticum Canticorum* 2.360 (*GCS*, Origen 8.113) writes, " 'fusca sum et formosa ...' In aliis exemplaribus legimus: 'nigra sum et formosa' " (I am dark and beautiful ... In some copies we read: I am black and beautiful); and most of the early commentators read "and" (see Snowden, *Blacks in Antiquity*, p. 331, n. 17). But Courtès, "The Theme of 'Ethiopia,' " in his discussion of the Origen commentary (p. 14) apparently cites the *sed* (but) reading of the Vulgate 1:4 ("nigra sum, sed formosa").

213. Origen *Commentarium in Canticum Canticorum* 2.360 (*GCS*, Origen 8.113).

214. Ibid. 2.360–361 (*GCS*, Origen 8.113–114).

215. Antiphon, frg. 44; K. Freeman, *Ancilla to the Pre-Socratic Philosophers* (Cambridge, Mass. 1962) p. 148.

216. Numbers 12.1–16; *Commentarium in Canticum Canticorum* 2.362 (*GCS*, Origen 8.115); 2.366–367 (*GCS*, Origen 8.117–118).

217. Origen 2.367–369 (*GCS*, 8.118–119); Matthew 12.42 and 1 Kings 10.1–10.

218. Origen 2.364 (*GCS*, 8.116) and 2.372 (*GCS*, 8.122); Psalms 67.31, LXX as cited by Origen.

219. Origen 2.364–365 (*GCS*, 8.116); cf. Sophonias 3.10, LXX as cited by Origen.

220. Origen 2.365 (*GCS*, 8.117).

221. Diodorus 3.2–3.1.

222. Ps-Callisthenes *Historia Alexandri Magni* 3.18.6 in W. Kroll's ed. (Berlin 1926) I, 116; L. Bergson, *Der griechische Alexanderroman Rezension B* (Stockholm, Göteborg, Uppsala 1965) 3.18.10–11, p. 153.

223. W. Peek, *Griechische Vers-Inschriften* (Berlin 1955) no. 1167.

224. Origen *Commentarium in Canticum Canticorum* 2.377 (*GCS*, Origen 8.125–126).

225. Origen 2.379 (*GCS*, 8.127).

226. Origen *Homiliae in Canticum Canticorum* 1.6 (*GCS*, Origen 8.36). On the theme of blackness, Ethiopians, and sin in writers of the early centuries after Christ, see Courtès, pp. 27–28, and Devisse, pp. 61–62, in *Image of the Black in Western Art*, II, pt. 1.

227. Gregory of Nyssa *Commentarium in Canticum Canticorum* (1,5–6) oratio 2 (*PG* 44.792), ed. W. Jaeger, VI [Leiden 1960] p. 51; cf. Psalms 87.4–5.

228. Cyril of Alexandria *Expositio in Psalmos* 73.14 (*PG* 69.1188); cf. Psalms 71.9 (LXX), 72.9 (*RSV*); 73.14 (LXX), 74.14 (*RSV*); and Sophonias 2.12.

229. Jerome *Commentarii in Sophoniam prophetam* 2.12ff. (*PL* 25.1367–1369); cf. Jeremiah 13.23; Song of Songs 8.5 (LXX).

230. Augustine *Enarrationes in Psalmos* 73.16 *CCL* 39.1014; cf. Ephesians 5.8.

231. Acts 8.26–40. "Eunuch" in this instance is perhaps not to be taken literally but may be used in the sense of a high court official; C. Brown, ed. *The New International Dictionary of New Testament Theology* (Exeter 1975), p. 560.

232. H. J. Cadbury, *The Book of Acts in History* (New York 1955) p. 15.

233. John Chrysostom *Homiliae in Epistulam Primam ad Corinthios* 36.6 (*PG* 61.314–315).

234. Jerome *Epistulae* 69.6.7–8.

235. Theodoret *Interpretatio in Psalmos* 67.32 (*PG* 80.1397).

236. Rufinus *Historia ecclesiastica* 1.9 (*PL* 21.478–480; Socrates *Historia ecclesiastica* 1.19 (*PG* 67.125–130); Sozomen *Historia ecclesiastica* 2.24 (*PG* 67.996–1000); Gelasius *Historia ecclesiastica* 3.9.3–17 (*GCS* 28.148–150).

237. Palladius *Historia Lausiaca* 52 (*PG* 34.1145C; Rufinus of Aquileia *Historia monachorum, de Apollonio* 7.151 (*PL* 21.415). Courtès, "The Theme of 'Ethiopia,' " p. 21, questions whether the report of the monks should be taken as actual fact, and then adds that though the possibility is there, "it seems more likely that at the same time the narrator is expressing repentance for his antiracial feelings by a kind of rhetorical paradox." Similarly Courtès (p. 25 and p. 211, n. 59) casts doubt on the existence of Abba Moses (below, note 243). Both the monks and Moses are in the classical tradition of pious Ethiopians, favorites of the gods. Even if the accounts are completely apocryphal, they (especially the full reports of Moses) are an important part in the formation of the early Christian image of Ethiopians.

238. The fresco is in Warsaw, Muzeum Narodowe, 234031; T. Dzier-

zykray-Rogalski, "Remarques sur la typologie anthropologique des fresques de Faras (Pachoras)," in *Mélanges offerts à Kazimierz Michalowski* (Warsaw 1966) pp. 83–86; S. Jakobielski, *Faras III: A History of the Bishopric of Pachoras on the Basis of Coptic Inscriptions* (Warsaw 1972) p. 129; *Africa in Antiquity,* II, 326, fig. 292, and illustration on p. 327.

239. Augustine *Enarrationes in Psalmos* 71.12 (*CCL* 39.980).

240. Fulgentius *Epistulae* 11–12 (*PL* 65.378–392).

241. Augustine *Enarrationes* 67.41 (*CCL* 39.898).

242. For a recent discussion of the ampullae depicting Menas as a Negro, see Devisse, *Image of the Black in Western Art,* II, pt. 1, pp. 38–43, and the literature cited there. The appearance of Menas as a Negro of the "pure" type on several ampullae (e.g. Oxford, Ashmolean Museum, 1933.717; Paris, Musée du Louvre, MNC 140) has puzzled scholars, and a number of explanations have been offered, including Devisse's unconvincing suggestion (p. 43) that "the canny monks 'met the need' manifested by their black clientele by giving their saint, as occasion demanded, a black face exportable all through the Nile Valley toward the south." Egypt, where blacks and whites had lived side by side for centuries and worshiped Isis at the same temple, was an environment compatible with a tradition of a black Menas.

243. For sources of the life of Abba Moses, see Palladius *Historia Lausiaca* 22 (*PG* 34.1065–1068); Sozomen *Historica ecclesiastica* 6.29 (*PG* 67.1376–1381); *Acta Sanctorum,* August, VI 199–212; *Apophthegmata Patrum* (*PG* 65.281–290); *Vita S. Moysis Aethiopis* in V. Latyshev, *Menologii anonymi Byzantini saeculi X quae supersunt* (St. Petersburg 1912) fasc. 2, pp. 330–336; H. G. Evelyn-White, *The Monasteries of the Wâdi' N' Natrun,* II: *The History of the Monasteries of Nitria and of Scetis* (New York 1932) pp. 154–156; *Image of the Black in Western Art,* II, pt. 1, pp. 25, 62, 113, 225, nn. 256–257. P. Mayerson, "Anti-Black Sentiment in the *Vitae Patrum,*" *Harvard Theological Review* 71 (1978) 304–311, regards references to black or Ethiopian demons and to the color of Abba Moses as evidence of anti-black sentiment—evidence he describes (p. 304) as "not one of highly articulated prejudice," but "neither overly subtle nor subliminal." On p. 307 he characterizes the use of color words in certain contexts relating to Abba Moses (e.g. *Apophthegmata Patrum, PG* 65.284, the episode in which Moses, clad in his white vestment at the time of his ordination, wondered whether he was as white inwardly as he was outwardly) as "the equivalent of the most offensive word used against blacks in American society." Courtès, "The Theme of 'Ethiopia' and 'Ethiopians,' " p. 62, states that such episodes in the life of Moses should be interpreted allegorically, and concludes that "the person of Abba Moses seems to epitomize the *Aethiops-*

sinner's symbolic road from the darkness of sin to the light of grace" (cf. Snowden, *Blacks in Antiquity*, pp. 201, 209–211).

244. On the importance of this event, see Courtès, "The Theme of 'Ethiopia,' " p. 21.

245. Quodvultdeus, *Livre des promesses et des prédictions de Dieu*, ed. R. Braun, I (Paris 1964), no. 101 *Sources chrétiennes*, 2.9.15, p. 328. Quodvultdeus reads "Fusca sum et decora," which Courtès, "The Theme of 'Ethiopia," p. 31, incorrectly translates as "but"; cf. his citation of Origen's reading of the same passage (above, note 212). For the attribution to Quodvultdeus and the date (between 445 and 455), see pp. 107–113 and 15–18.

246. Arator, *De Actibus Apostolorum* 1.673–707, *CSEL* 72.52–54.

247. The potentiality of the ancient black-white imagery for vastly different uses has been the subject of frequent comment. J. Desanges, "L'Antiquité gréco-romaine et l'homme noir," *Revue d'études latines*, 48 (1970) 53, states that the association of blackness with death, the Underworld, and evil contained the germs of uneasy developments that antiquity was able to overcome. B. M. Warmington, reviewing Snowden, *Blacks in Antiquity* in *African Historical Studies* 4.2 (1971) 93, writes that even if the black-bad, white-good equation had nothing to do with the color of the skin, "one cannot altogether avoid a *frisson* of unease at a constant harping on the distinction between physical blackness and spiritual whiteness, innocent though it was in early Christian writing." Such observations underscore a most noteworthy aspect of the attitude toward color in antiquity: the ability of the ancients to see and comment on the obviously different physical characteristics of peoples without equating inferiority or superiority with skin color. The changing roles of black-white imagery in the gradual development of racism in postclassical societies is a subject that needs further investigation.

248. K. Irvine, *The Rise of the Colored Races* (New York 1970) p. 19.

249. With respect to the factors that may have shaped the white-black pattern in antiquity, it is instructive to take note of some of the points made by W. B. Cohen, *The French Encounter with Africans,* in his explanation of the presence of color prejudice among the French, which, he argues, has persisted since earliest times: the initial negative image of blacks (pp. 1–6), reinforced by the experience of most Frenchmen who came to know blacks as slaves (pp. 35, 59); the equation of nègre with slave (p. 132); the laws against miscegenation (p. 51) and the abhorrence with which interracial marriages were generally regarded (p. 113); the negative opinion of Africans among thinkers of the Enlightenment (p. 67) with one notable exception (p. 68), and a slight modification deriving from the myth of the Noble Savage

(p. 70); the hierarchical notion of human races, with Europeans occupying the highest and Africans the lowest position (p. 76); scientific racism in the nineteenth century and Gobineau's synthesis of nineteenth-century French racial thinking (pp. 210–238); the negative view of African religion, the resistance of blacks to Christianity, and the failure of Christianity in Africa resulting from a view of blacks as perverse and depraved (pp. 15–21). The striking contrasts between the French-black and the ancient black-white patterns outlined in this study provide a significant commentary on the different approaches to blacks in the ancient and modern worlds.

250. Colossians 3:11. Also Galatians 3:28: "There is no such thing as Jew and Greek, slave and freeman, male and female; for you are all one person in Christ Jesus." See H. C. Baldry, *The Unity of Mankind in Greek Thought* (Cambridge, Eng. 1965), for a history of the distinctions that the Greeks made on the basis of sex, birth, slave and free, Greek and barbarian.

SOURCES OF ILLUSTRATIONS

1–2. Boston, Museum of Fine Arts, Department of Egyptian and Near Eastern Art, 14.718 and 14.719. Photos Museum of Fine Arts, Harvard/MFA Expedition.

3. New York, Metropolitan Museum of Art, 66.78, gift of Mrs. William Sergeant Kendall and Mrs. Daniel Crena de Iongh, 1966. Photo Metropolitan Museum of Art.

4. Cairo, Egyptian Museum, JE 51730. Photo Egyptian Museum.

5a-b. Cairo, Egyptian Museum, JE 30969. Photos Menil Foundation/Mario Carrieri, Milan.

6. St. Louis, St. Louis Art Museum, 18:1940. Photo St. Louis Art Museum.

7a-b. London, British Museum, Department of Egyptian Antiquities, 921, 922. Photos Trustees of the British Museum.

8a-b. Thebes, necropolis of Qurnet Murai. Photos Menil Foundation/Mario Carrieri, Milan.

9. Cairo, Egyptian Museum, JE 36677 (CG 42010). Photo Menil Foundation/Mario Carrieri, Milan.

10. Copenhagen, Ny Carlsberg Glyptotek, AEIN 1538. Photo Ny Carlsberg Glyptotek.

11. London, British Museum, Department of Egyptian Antiquities, 1770. Photo Trustees of the British Museum.

12. London, British Museum, Department of Western Asiatic Antiquities, BM 127412. Photo Trustees of the British Museum.

13. London, British Museum, 124928. Photo Trustees of the British Museum.

14. Oxford, Ashmolean Museum, Department of Antiquities, 1938.537. Photo Ashmolean Museum.

15. West Berlin, Antikenmuseum, Staatliche Museen, V.I. 3250. Photo Antikenmuseum.

16. Boston, Museum of Fine Arts, 00.332, Pierce Fund. Photo Museum of Fine Arts.

17. Boston, Museum of Fine Arts, Department of Classical Art, 63.2663, Arthur Tracy Cabot Fund. Photo Museum of Fine Arts.

18. Oxford, Ashmolean Museum, Department of Antiquities, 1888.216. Photo Ashmolean Museum.

19. Athens, National Museum, 9683. Photo National Museum.

20. West Berlin, Antikenmuseum, Staatliche Museen, F 2534. Photo Antikenmuseum.

21. East Berlin, Staatliche Museen zu Berlin, Antikensammlung, 3237. Photo Staatliche Museen zu Berlin.

22a-b. Oxford, Ashmolean Museum, Department of Antiquities, G 97. Photos Ashmolean Museum.

23. London, British Museum, Department of Greek and Roman Antiquities, 1955.10-8.1. Photo Trustees of the British Museum.

24. Providence, Museum of Art, Rhode Island School of Design, 11.035, gift of Mrs. Gustav Radeke. Photo Museum of Art, Rhode Island School of Design.

25a-b. Boston, Museum of Fine Arts, Department of Classical Art, 96.698, Perkins Collection. Photos Museum of Fine Arts and Menil Foundation/Hickey and Robertson, Houston.

26. Tunis, Musée National du Bardo, 3361. Photo Musée National du Bardo.

27a-b. Janiform vase: Boston, Museum of Fine Arts, Department of Classical Art, 98.888. Photo Museum of Fine Arts. Shilluk: From C. S. Coon, *The Origin of Races* (New York: Alfred A. Knopf, 1962), plate 4, photograph by Lidio Cipriani.

28a-b. Head-vase: Florence, Museo Archeologico, 2288. Photo Soprintendenza Archeologica della Toscana-Firenze. Somali: From C. S. Coon, with E. E. Hunt, Jr., *The Living Races of Man* (New York: Alfred A. Knopf, 1965), plate 123, photograph by Lidio Cipriani.

29a-b. East Berlin, Staatliche Museen zu Berlin, Antikensammlung, BR 10485-10486. Photos Staatliche Museen zu Berlin.

30. Formerly David M. Robinson Collection, present whereabouts un-

known. Photo University Museums, University of Mississippi Cultural Center.

31a-b. London, British Museum, Department of Coins and Medals, S.N.G. II (Lloyd) 31. Photos Trustees of the British Museum.

32a,b,c. Tunis, Musée National du Bardo. Photos Musée National du Bardo.

33. Rome, Palazzo Rondinini. Photo Banca Nazionale dell' Agricoltura and Deutsches Archäologisches Institut, Rome.

34. New York, Norbert Schimmel Collection. Photo Norbert Schimmel Collection.

35. Cairo, Egyptian Museum, JE 62045. Photo Menil Foundation/Mario Carrieri, Milan.

36. Boston, Museum of Fine Arts, Department of Egyptian and Near Eastern Art, 03.1567–1574, Sears Fund. Photo Museum of Fine Arts.

37. Brooklyn, Brooklyn Museum, Department of Egyptian and Classical Art, 37.413, Charles Edwin Wilbour Fund. Photo Brooklyn Museum.

38. West Berlin, Ägyptisches Museum, 21834. Photo Ägyptisches Museum.

39a-b. Plovdiv, National Archaeological Museum, 3204. Photo Menil Foundation/Mario Carrieri, Milan.

40a-b. East Berlin, Staatliche Museen zu Berlin, Münzkabinett, Prokesch-Osten Collection, 1875. Photos Staatliche Museen zu Berlin.

41. Collection of the author.

42. Paris, Musée du Louvre, Département des Antiquités Grecques et Romaines, N3408. Photo Musée du Louvre.

43. London, British Museum, Department of Greek and Roman Antiquities, 1893.3-3.1. Photo Trustees of the British Museum.

44. West Berlin, Antikenmuseum, Staatliche Museen, TC 8626. Photo Antikenmuseum.

45. Oxford, Ashmolean Museum, Department of Antiquities, 1884.583. Photo Ashmolean Museum.

46. Cambridge, Mass., The Arthur M. Sackler Museum, Harvard University, 1960.327, bequest of David M. Robinson. Photo The Arthur M. Sackler Museum.

47. Brooklyn, Brooklyn Museum, Department of Ancient Art, 67.70, Charles Edwin Wilbour Fund. Photo Brooklyn Museum.

48a,b,c. Paris, Bibliothèque Nationale, Cabinet des Médailles. Photos Menil Foundation/Hickey and Robertson, Houston.

49. Boston, Museum of Fine Arts, Department of Classical Art, 88.643, Benjamin Pierce Cheney Donation. Photo Museum of Fine Arts.

50a-b. Brooklyn, Brooklyn Museum, Department of Ancient Art, 70.59,

Charles Edwin Wilbour Fund. Photos Brooklyn Museum.

51. El Djem, Musée Archéologique. Photo Menil Foundation/Mario Carrieri, Milan.

52. Tunis, Musée National du Bardo, A105. Photo Musée National du Bardo.

53. Musée du Louvre, Département des Antiquités Grecques et Romaines, MA 1796. Photo Musée du Louvre.

54. Sfax, Musée de Sfax. Photo Musée National du Bardo.

55. Tunis, Musée National du Bardo, A19. Photo Musée National du Bardo.

56. Sfax, Musée de Sfax. Photo Musée National du Bardo.

57. Toronto, Royal Ontario Museum, 959.17.15. Photo Royal Ontario Museum.

58. Cherchell, Musée Archéologique, 21. Photo Menil Foundation/Mario Carrieri, Milan.

59. Boston, Museum of Fine Arts, 63.2663, Arthur Tracy Cabot Fund. Photo Museum of Fine Arts.

60. Naples, Museo Archeologico Nazionale, 8924. Photo Alinari/Editorial Photocolor Archives.

61. Naples, Museo Archeologico Nazionale, 8919. Photo Alinari/Editorial Photocolor Archives.

62. Oxford, Ashmolean Museum, 1888.315. Photo Ashmolean Museum.

INDEX